DEFINING MOMENTS

THE ZOOT SUIT RIOTS

DEFINING MOMENTS

THE ZOOT SUIT RIOTS

Kevin Hillstrom

Omnigraphics

155 W. Congress, Suite 200
Detroit, MI 48226

Omnigraphics, Inc.

Kevin Hillstrom, *Series Editor*
Cherie D. Abbey, *Managing Editor*

Peter E. Ruffner, *Publisher*
Matthew P. Barbour, *Senior Vice President*

Elizabeth Collins, *Research and Permissions Coordinator*
Kevin M. Hayes, *Operations Manager*

Mary Butler, *Researcher*
Cherry Edwards, *Permissions Assistant*
Shirley Amore, Joseph Harris, Martha Johns, and Kirk Kauffmann, *Administrative Staff*

ISBN 978-0-7808-1285-7

Library of Congress Cataloging-in-Publication Data

Hillstrom, Kevin, 1963-
The Zoot Suit Riots / by Kevin Hillstrom.
p. cm. — (Defining moments)
Includes bibliographical references and index.
Summary: "Surveys the political events, social trends, and racial attitudes that contributed to a week-long outbreak of violence in Los Angeles in 1943 by white servicemen and civilians against young Mexican-American 'zoot suiters.' Includes a narrative overview, biographies, primary sources, chronology, glossary, bibliography, and index"—Provided by publisher.
ISBN 978-0-7808-1285-7 (hardcover : acid-free paper) 1. Zoot Suit Riots, Los Angeles, Calif., 1943. 2. Mexican Americans—California—Los Angeles—Social conditions—20th century. 3. Violence—California—Los Angeles—History—20th century. 4. Los Angeles (Calif.)—Race relations. 5. Los Angeles (Calif.)—Social conditions—20th century. I. Title.
F869.L89M447 2012
306.09794'94053—dc23 2012029556

Printed in the United States of America

TABLE OF CONTENTS

PRIMARY SOURCES

PREFACE

Throughout the course of America's existence, its people, culture, and institutions have been periodically challenged—and in many cases transformed—by profound historical events. Some of these momentous events, such as women's suffrage, the civil rights movement, and U.S. involvement in World War II, invigorated the nation and strengthened American confidence and capabilities. Others, such as the Great Depression, the Vietnam War, and Watergate, have prompted troubled assessments and heated debates about the country's core beliefs and character.

Some of these defining moments in American history were years or even decades in the making. The Harlem Renaissance and the New Deal, for example, unfurled over the span of several years, while the American labor movement and the Cold War evolved over the course of decades. Other defining moments, such as the Cuban missile crisis and the Japanese attack on Pearl Harbor, transpired over a matter of days or weeks.

But although significant differences exist among these events in terms of their duration and their place in the timeline of American history, all share the same basic characteristic: they transformed the United States' political, cultural, and social landscape for future generations of Americans.

Taking heed of this fundamental reality, American citizens, schools, and other institutions are increasingly emphasizing the importance of understanding our nation's history. Omnigraphics' *Defining Moments* series was created for the express purpose of meeting this growing appetite for authoritative, useful historical resources. This series will be of enduring value to anyone interested in learning more about America's past—and in understanding how those historical events continue to reverberate in the twenty-first century.

Each individual volume of *Defining Moments* provides a valuable resource for readers interested in learning about the most profound events in our nation's history. Each volume is organized into three distinct sections—Narrative Overview, Biographies, and Primary Sources.

- The **Narrative Overview** provides readers with a detailed, factual account of the origins and progression of the "defining moment" being examined. It also explores the event's lasting impact on America's political and cultural landscape.
- The **Biographies** section provides valuable biographical background on leading figures associated with the event in question. Each biography concludes with a list of sources for further information on the profiled individual.
- The **Primary Sources** section collects a wide variety of pertinent primary source materials from the era under discussion, including official documents, papers and resolutions, letters, oral histories, memoirs, editorials, and other important works.

Individually, each of these sections is a rich resource for users. Together, they comprise an authoritative, balanced, and absorbing examination of some of the most significant events in U.S. history.

Other notable features contained within each volume in the series include a glossary of important individuals, places, and terms; a detailed chronology featuring page references to relevant sections of the narrative; an annotated bibliography of sources for further study; an extensive general bibliography that reflects the wide range of historical sources consulted by the author; and a subject index.

New Feature—Research Topics for Student Reports

Each volume in the *Defining Moments* series now includes a list of potential research topics for students. Students working on historical research and writing assignments will find this feature especially useful in assessing their options.

Information on the highlighted research topics can be found throughout the different sections of the book—and especially in the narrative overview, biography, and primary source sections. This wide coverage gives readers the flexibility to study the topic through multiple entry points.

Acknowledgements

This series was developed in consultation with a distinguished Advisory Board comprised of public librarians, school librarians, and educators. They evaluated the series as it developed, and their comments and suggestions were invaluable throughout the production process. Any errors in this and other volumes in the series are ours alone. Following is a list of board members who contributed to the *Defining Moments* series:

Comments and Suggestions

We welcome your comments on *Defining Moments: The Zoot Suit Riots* and suggestions for other events in U.S. history that warrant treatment in the *Defining Moments* series. Correspondence should be addressed to:

Editor, *Defining Moments*
Omnigraphics, Inc.
P.O. Box 31-1640
Detroit, MI 48231
E-mail: editorial@omnigraphics.com

HOW TO USE THIS BOOK

Defining Moments: The Zoot Suit Riots provides users with a detailed and authoritative overview of this pivotal episode in U.S. history. The preparation and arrangement of this volume—and all other books in the *Defining Moments* series—reflect an emphasis on providing a thorough and objective account of events that shaped our nation, presented in an easy-to-use reference work.

The Zoot Suit Riots is divided into three main sections. The first of these sections, **Narrative Overview**, surveys the political events, social trends, and racial attitudes that contributed to a week-long outbreak of violence in 1943 by white servicemen and civilians against young Mexican-American "zoot suiters." This overview provides extensive coverage of the riots themselves, as well as the 1942 Sleepy Lagoon murder trial, which has been cited as an important contributor to the outbreak of the riots. But the narrative also sets the Zoot Suit Riots within the context of the wider Latino-American experience. To that end, it details Hispanic-American history from the colonial era to the present, devoting particular attention to high-interest topics like illegal immigration, heritage preservation, and the Latino community's growing economic and political power in twenty-first century America.

The second section, **Biographies**, provides complete, authoritative biographical profiles of leading figures associated with the Sleepy Lagoon trial and the Zoot Suit Riots. Featured individuals include Henry "Hank" Leyvas, the purported "ringleader" of the Hispanic-American youth who were convicted in the Sleepy Lagoon case; Charles William Fricke, the Sleepy Lagoon judge whose hostility to the defense in that trial became legendary; Alice Greenfield, a social justice activist and leading advocate for the Sleepy Lagoon defendants; and Fletcher Bowron, the law-and-order mayor of Los Angeles who refused to admit that racial prejudice had anything to do with the Zoot Suit Riots.

The third section, **Primary Sources**, collects essential and illuminating documents on the Zoot Suit Riots. These documents include excerpts from transcripts of the contentious Sleepy Lagoon murder trial; a short story about the Zoot Suit Riots from someone who witnessed the mob violence firsthand; racially inflammatory news stories and editorials about Mexican Americans in the Los Angeles press before, during, and after the riots; an assessment of the Zoot Suit Riots from a group of concerned citizens of Los Angeles; and modern perspectives on the status of Latino Americans in the twenty-first century.

Other valuable features in *Defining Moments: The Zoot Suit Riots* include the following:

- Attribution and referencing of primary sources and other quoted material to help guide users to other valuable historical research resources.
- Glossary of Important People, Places, and Terms.
- Detailed Chronology of events includes references to page numbers within the Narrative Overview wherein users can find additional information on the event in question.
- Photographs of the leading figures and major events associated with the Sleepy Lagoon murder trial and the Zoot Suit Riots.
- Sources for Further Study, an annotated list of noteworthy works about Hispanic-American life in the United States.
- Extensive bibliography of works consulted in the creation of this book, including books, periodicals, and Internet sites.
- A Subject Index.

Note: People of Mexican and/or Latino descent who live and work in the United States have been referred to by a wide range of terms over the years, including Mexican American, Chicano, Hispanic, and Latino. In this historical overview, the author has generally used the dominant terminology of the period under discussion (i.e., "Mexican American" in discussions of events in California and other parts of the American West in the pre-World War II era). The terms are used more interchangeably in the book's discussions of more recent events.

RESEARCH TOPICS FOR DEFINING MOMENTS: THE ZOOT SUIT RIOTS

When students receive an assignment to produce a research paper on a historical event or topic, the first step in that process—settling on a subject for the paper—can also be one of the most vexing. In recognition of that reality, each book in the *Defining Moments* series now highlights research areas/topics that receive extensive coverage within that particular volume.

Potential research topics for students using *Defining Moments: The Zoot Suit Riots* include the following:

- Investigate the important role that bloodlines played in determining one's social and economic status in the Spanish Empire.
- Explain the political, cultural, and economic factors that contributed to the mass migration of Mexicans into the United States in the nineteenth and early twentieth centuries.
- Show how economic trends and events in the United States have historically influenced American attitudes toward migrant workers from Mexico and other countries.
- Explain the impact that newspapers and other information sources had on white attitudes toward Mexican Americans in general (and zoot suiters specifically) both before and during the Zoot Suit Riots.
- Detail reasons why zoot suits emerged as such a popular fashion style in minority and working-class neighborhoods across America in the 1930s.
- Explore the history of mass trials such as the Sleepy Lagoon trial, and the reasons why such trials have fallen out of favor since the 1940s.
- Explain the importance of Mexican-American, African-American, and other minority World War II veterans in changing American attitudes about integration and racial equality during the 1940s and 1950s.

- Explain the historical development of—and current debates about—terms such as Chicano, Hispanic, and Latino that are used to denote people with ancestral ties to Mexico and other parts of Latin America.
- Identify one major challenge facing Hispanic-American families and communities today and summarize proposed solutions to that problem.

NARRATIVE OVERVIEW

PROLOGUE

From a distance the downtown streets of Los Angeles looked and sounded like they always did on summertime evenings during World War II. Lights from nightclubs, restaurants, and movie houses illuminated the night, shining down on passing automobiles and pedestrians. The sidewalks teemed with civilians, police officers, and knots of fast-walking sailors, the latter hailing from naval bases that perched on the city's outskirts. The air was full of music and shouting and the rumble and swish of moving cars, jeeps, streetcars, and buses.

Any visitor approaching closer, however, would have quickly realized that the atmosphere on those streets was anything but relaxed. Instead, the air was suffused with a frantic energy and nervous tension that enveloped the entire downtown district and nearby neighborhoods. A keen observer would have also noticed that some of the servicemen were clutching pipes, bats, and other rough weapons in their hands—and that many of the armed servicemen were rushing in and out of the shining doors of the downtown establishments with bursts of loud exclamations, as if they were frustrated hunters tracking down prized game. Finally, if the visitor lingered long enough, he or she might have learned that the sailors *were* on the hunt. But their quarry was not rabbit, deer, or pheasant. They were after Mexican-American zoot suiters, young men whose colorful choice of wardrobe had somehow made them walking and talking symbols of juvenile delinquency and immorality to many white Angelenos.

One of the observers who journeyed to the heart of downtown Los Angeles to bear witness to these events was Al Waxman, editor of a small Jewish newspaper called the *Eastside Journal*. Waxman saw many disturbing sights during the course of the so-called Zoot Suit Riots, which replayed nightly in the streets of Los Angeles for more than a week in June 1943. But for him, the fifth night of the riots—June 7—was the worst:

> At Twelfth and Central I came upon a scene that will long live in my memory. Police were swinging clubs and servicemen were fighting with [Mexican] civilians. Wholesale arrests were being made by the officers.
>
> Four boys came out of a pool hall. They were wearing the zoot suits that have become the symbol of a fighting flag. Police ordered them into arrest cars. One refused. He asked: "Why am I being arrested?" The police officer answered with three swift blows of the night-stick across the boy's head and he went down. As he sprawled, he was kicked in the face. Police had difficulty loading his body into the vehicle because he was one-legged and wore a wooden limb. Maybe the officer didn't know he was attacking a cripple.
>
> At the next corner a Mexican mother cried out, "Don't take my boy, he did nothing. He's only fifteen years old. Don't take him." She was struck across the jaw with a night-stick and almost dropped the two and a half year old baby that was clinging in her arms....
>
> Rushing back to the east side to make sure that things were quiet here, I came upon a band of servicemen making a systematic tour of East First Street. They had just come out of a cocktail bar where four men were nursing bruises. Three autos loaded with Los Angeles policemen were on the scene but the soldiers were not molested. Farther down the street the men stopped a streetcar, forcing the motorman to open the door and proceeded to inspect the clothing of the male passengers. "We're looking for zoot suits to burn," they shouted. Again the police did not interfere.... Half a block away ... I pleaded with the men of the local police substation to put a stop to these activities. "It is a matter for the military police," they said....[1]

Today, the Zoot Suit Riots are widely described as an embarrassing chapter in the history of both the city of Los Angeles and the state of California. Historians describe those ugly spasms of violence as a grim reminder of the racial discrimination and fear that saturated America prior to the civil rights movement of the 1960s. Yet the riots are also described as a historic turning point for Hispanic Americans. As they surveyed the physical and emotional wreckage of that horrible week, they began charting a new path for themselves. This path has been rocky and harrowing at times. But as many modern-day Hispanic Americans will attest, it has also brought them to a point where the American promise of "life, liberty, and the pursuit of happiness," long enshrined in the Declaration of Independence, finally applies to them as well.

Note:

[1] Waxman, Al. Quoted in *North from Mexico* by Carey McWilliams. Philadelphia: J.B. Lippincott Co., 1949, p. 249.

Chapter One

CAUGHT IN THE CURRENTS OF EMPIRE AND CONQUEST

> On our western & southern frontiers, Spain holds an immense country, the occupancy of which, however, is in the Indian natives, except a few insulated spots possessed by Spanish subjects.... It is impossible not to look forward to distant times, when our rapid multiplication will expand itself beyond those limits, & cover the whole northern, if not the southern continent, with a people speaking the same language, governed in similar forms, & by similar laws.
>
> —Thomas Jefferson, letter to James Monroe, November 24, 1801

When Italian explorer Christopher Columbus convinced the kingdom of Spain to bankroll his search for an ocean route to Asia in the late fifteenth century, it set in motion a chain of events that forever altered the path of numerous civilizations around the world. Columbus's 1492 discovery of the Americas—the so-called New World—ushered in a great age of European exploration and empire-building. Spain was at the forefront of this era of conquest. Its armies of *conquistadores* (conquerors) demolished the native societies of Central and South America and established a vast colonial empire in their place.

Ancient Native Civilizations of the Americas

Historians believe that when European expeditions first arrived in the New World in the late 1400s and early 1500s, the Americas already contained somewhere between 60 million and 100 million people. Many parts of the continents were only lightly populated, but a few regions featured advanced civilizations with large populations of native Indians. South America's Andes Mountains, for example, was home to the Inca Empire, which encompassed six to twelve million people.

Further north, the Mayan Empire may have had an even greater population at one time. This civilization was based in modern-day Mexico's Yucatan Peninsula. At the height of its glory—a period that extended from about 250-900 A.D.—the Mayan Empire encompassed about forty major cities adorned with great plazas, temples, and pyramids. By the time Europeans discovered the New World, however, the Mayan civilization was already in steep decline.

The third of the great city-states of America in the pre-Columbian era (the historical period before Columbus's arrival) was the Aztec Empire. The Aztec capital of Tenochtitlán, which was based in the heart of the Valley of Mexico, supported an estimated quarter-million people all by itself. Its surrounding territory contained millions more.

These great empires went to war at various times to expand their holdings, and slavery was woven deeply into the fabric of both the Mayan and Aztec civilizations. Aztec religious beliefs also called for frequent human sacrifices to their gods. These kingdoms, though, also featured what one scholar described as "monumental architecture, brilliant artistic achievements, mathematics more sophisticated than those of Europe at the time, highly accurate astronomy, and the development of an unwieldy but functional form of writing."[1]

The early Spanish conquistadores were dazzled by the order and majesty of these civilizations. When Spanish explorer Hernándo Cortés took his army into Tenochtitlán for the first time in November 1519, one of his captains admitted that they were stunned by the city's architecture, which "looked like gleaming white towers and castles: a marvelous sight." The captain added that "some of our soldiers who had been in many parts of the world, in Constantinople, in Rome, and all over Italy, said they had never seen a market so well laid out, so large, so orderly, and so full of people."[2] The Spaniards' high regard for the vitality and sophistication of the Inca and Aztec civilizations, though, did not stop them from embarking on a swift and ruthless campaign of conquest.

Conquerors from Across the Sea

The Spaniards came to the Americas at a time when Europe was just emerging from centuries of deadly wars, famines, and plagues. Many countries contributed to Europe's escape from this dark Medieval era, as scholars sometimes called it. Italy and France, for example, were the central pillars of the European Renaissance, an exciting period of artistic growth and intellectual achievement that spanned the fourteenth through seventeenth centuries. Portugal established profitable trade routes through southern Asia and founded early colonial outposts in Africa (unfortunately, the Portuguese used these outposts to initiate the transatlantic slave trade beginning in the mid-fifteenth century). Beginning in 1485, meanwhile, a succession of kings and queens known collectively as the Tudor monarchy presided over a century of relative peace and economic growth in England.

Spanish conquistador Hernándo Cortés

Down in the southwestern reaches of Europe, the kingdom of Spain was also revitalizing itself under King Ferdinand of Aragón and Queen Isabella of Castille. The two monarchs, each of whom had governed smaller regions of what is now modern-day Spain, married in 1469 in order to unite their kingdoms. Under their joint rule, Catholic Spaniards drove out the last remnants of the Moors, an Arab people who had forcibly occupied Spanish land for many centuries. This military crusade created multiple generations of hardened warriors among the Spanish people.

When Columbus returned to Spain from America in March 1493, the explorer's accounts of fertile valleys, beautiful natural harbors, exotic foods and spices, great deposits of gold, and peaceful natives fired the imagination of the Spanish rulers. Ships full of conquistadores sailed for the New World to claim those treasures for the Spanish Empire. When these early arrivals discovered gold and silver in Mexico and Peru in the early 1500s, Spain's campaign to conquer and colonize the Americas further intensified.

The first of the great Indian civilizations to fall to the conquistadores was the Aztec Empire. "Having bided their time, having waited for an opportune moment, the Spaniards came forth to slay us," reported one Aztec witness. "The blood of the young warriors ran like water; it gathered in pools."[3] In 1521 the final remnants of the Aztec Empire fell to a combined force of conquistadores and native tribesmen commanded by Cortés. Twelve years later, the Incas met the same fate at the hands of Spanish conquistadores led by Francisco Pizarro. The descendents of the once-mighty Mayan civilization held out the longest, but only because the early conquistadores were not that interested in gaining control of the Yucatan Peninsula. They were more focused on other regions known to contain large gold and silver deposits. By the mid-1500s, though, the Spanish flag also was flying over the ancestral lands of the Mayans.

Life in Colonial Spain

During the course of the sixteenth century, groups of Spanish conquistadores roamed far and wide across the western flank of South America, Central America, and the islands of the Caribbean. Spanish excursions led by Hernando de Soto, Francisco Vásquez de Coronado, and Juan Ponce de León also entered Mexico and various parts of what is now the southern United States. As these expeditions claimed the wilderness for Spain, they also gave Spanish names to hundreds of rivers, mountains, and other geographic features.

The Spanish explorers carried firearms, horses, and sophisticated military strategies that gave them enormous advantages over the natives. The Spaniards also brought strange and fearsome diseases like smallpox against which Amerindians—the native peoples who lived in North and South America prior to the arrival of Europeans—had no immunity. Native Indians were overwhelmed by the forces of war and disease, and the populations of many tribes plummeted. In the Caribbean, for example, historians believe that the native population on the island of Hispaniola (now shared by two nations, Haiti and the Dominican Republic) probably numbered somewhere between 500,000 and one million when Columbus arrived there in 1492. By 1520 European diseases and Spanish guns had reduced the native population to fewer than 20,000 people. In Mexico, meanwhile, scholar Carmen Bernand estimates that the native population fell from 30 million to 3 million in the four decades following Cortez's arrival in the region.[4]

The Spaniards also brought their own religious, cultural, and political traditions with them to the New World. They wasted little time imposing these

Spanish explorers carried out empire-building expeditions throughout the New World during the sixteenth and seventeenth centuries.

traditions on the vanquished Amerindians. As historian Earl Shorris wrote, "languages disappeared, a system of mathematics based on ten was instituted, old methods of agriculture were replaced, the diet changed, people were required to wear European clothing, and all the gods that could not be assimilated were broken and buried."[5]

The Spaniards also established permanent military garrisons and religious missions throughout their new colonies. These lonely outposts served multiple purposes. They became centers of trade with nearby Indian peoples, provided a base for Catholic missionaries who wanted to convert the natives to their faith, and served as a tangible symbol of the Spanish Crown's claim on the surrounding territory. Many of these missions crumbled and failed over time, but others became the foundation for San Antonio, El Paso, Tucson, San Diego, Los Angeles, San Francisco, and other major American cities.

Finally, the Spaniards imposed their own ideas about land ownership on the natives. Spanish governors dispersed vast tracts of land to the soldiers and settlers who were colonizing the Americas for Spain's greater glory. Officers received the largest grants, some of which gradually expanded into estates called

Spanish missions became the foundation for many major cities in North America. Mission Concepcion (pictured here), for example, became an early building block in the formation of San Antonio after it was established in the 1750s.

haciendas that spanned hundreds of square miles. The labor on these landholdings was provided by Indians, most of whom were treated as virtual slaves. As the sixteenth century progressed, the Indians were joined in the colonial mines, fields, and pasturelands by growing numbers of African slaves.

Subjects of the Spanish Crown

Historians are virtually unanimous in describing Spain's invasion of the New World as ruthlessly violent and merciless. After the conquistadores established their dominance, however, some Spaniards began to object to the "Indian genocide" that was being carried out by their countrymen in the Americas. Spanish missionary Bartolomé de Las Casas played a vital role in changing the attitudes of both the Crown and the Catholic Church toward the Amerindians.

Horrified by the atrocities that he witnessed against the natives, he returned to Spain and launched a public relations campaign against Indian enslavement that lasted throughout the 1520s and 1530s.

In 1542 Las Casas's efforts finally paid off with Spain's adoption of the so-called "New Laws of the Indies." These new colonial regulations and codes of governance recognized the Amerindians as free and equal subjects of the Spanish Crown. The introduction of these laws reduced the suffering of many natives. Others, however, did not see any meaningful changes to their lives. The owners of the great haciendas of the Americas ruled their domains as virtual kings. If they decided to ignore the new codes, there was little that their native laborers could do about it.

With each passing generation, though, the lines between the conquerors and the conquered became a little more blurred. For one thing, the Spaniards worked extremely hard to convert the indigenous tribes of America to Christianity. Catholic priests performed thousands of baptisms of natives at their missions. They also oversaw Catholic marriage ceremonies between wealthy Spaniards and Indians who were members of important tribal families. The children of these marriages of Spanish and Indian parents, known as *mestizos*, became an ever-growing percentage of the overall population.

New Racial Groups Emerge

Historians say that the Spaniards' openness to racial mixing with the native peoples of the New World was partly due to the fact that the first wave of colonists from Spain contained very low numbers of women. Another factor, though, was that "the Spanish people who sailed to the Americas were themselves the mestizos of Europe," in the words of Shorris. Over the previous centuries, he explained, they had already mixed with all sorts of nationalities of the ancient world, including "Celtic tribes, Phoenician sailors, soldiers and settlers from Carthage, Greeks, Hebrews, Romans, Visigoths, and Moors."[6]

This tradition of racial mixing reduced the social stigma of having sexual relations with Africans as well. In fact, Spanish colonists frequently engaged in sexual relations with people of African descent. These unions created a new racial group that the Spanish called *mulatos* (spelled "mulattoes" in English)—children with one African and one Spanish parent.

Official and unofficial unions between people of Spanish blood and people of African heritage became even more commonplace at the close of the eighteenth century. At that time, changes in Spanish colonial policies made it much easier for African slaves to purchase their freedom. As a result, free blacks and free mulattoes grew into major sectors of the population in the Spanish colonies. In Mexico, for example, the number of "free colored" outnumbered the slave population by about 60,000 to 10,000 by 1810. A similar ratio prevailed in Puerto Rico. By 1820 its slave population of 22,000 was one-fifth the size of its free colored population of 104,000.[7]

It would be inaccurate to say that mulattoes, mestizos, Indians, or free blacks in the Spanish colonies were treated as equals by rich landowners or colonial administrators, however. Most of these elites could trace their ancestry back to Spain and the original conquistadores. They did not much care whether lower-class white colonists married outside their race, but they were determined to keep their own bloodlines "pure." This attitude kept ownership of Spanish America's vast haciendas, which were handed down from generation to generation, in the hands of the *peninsulars* (Spaniards born in Spain) and the *creoles* (people born of Spanish parents in the Americas).

By 1800 an estimated 13.5 million people were living in Spanish America. Only about three million were whites of unmixed Spanish descent, though—and only 200,000 or so were actual peninsulars. This tiny upper class enforced a rigid caste system in the Americas. Their system of ethnic classification preserved the place of peninsulars at the top of colonial society and kept Indians and blacks at the bottom. The caste system also gave varying levels of preferential treatment to creoles, mestizos, and *castizos* (people who had one Spanish parent and one mestizo parent). "What did these terms mean?" asks historian Maria-Elena Martinez. "Well, it could determine whether you could be a priest, whether you could enter the university, whether you could enter religious guilds, ... whether you could become a nun. In other words, the terms had actual social consequences and, taken as a whole, they were meant to create this hierarchical society based on ancestry, based on blood."[8]

The Spanish Empire Comes Crashing Down

The Spaniards believed that they were building an empire in the western hemisphere that would forever glorify the Spanish Crown and the Catholic Church. They also were confident that the Indians whose land they had taken would never rise up against Spanish rule. For many years this confidence seemed justified, despite occasional rebellions like a 1680 uprising that Pueblo Indians mounted against Spanish rule in modern-day New Mexico.

In the early nineteenth century, however, a flurry of independence movements across the Americas brought the empire crashing down. These rebellions had their roots in long-simmering resentments about the Spaniards' exploitation of Indian lands and peoples for profit, as well as the discriminatory caste system imposed by the peninsulars. These resentments might not have exploded into calls for independence, though, were it not for events that took place thousands of miles away.

Simón Bolivar of Venezuela led several wars of rebellion against Spanish colonialism in the early nineteenth century.

The first of these events was the Revolutionary War in America. When the thirteen British colonies in America took up arms and cast off English rule in 1783, the great mass of poor and disinherited people living in the Spanish Empire took notice. They realized that independence from European colonialism might be possible for them as well.

The most important factor in the fall of Spanish America, though, was the onset of a series of wars in Europe. These so-called Napoleonic Wars (so named because French general Napoleon Bonaparte instigated much of the violence) brought down the Spanish Crown in 1808. When the Spanish colonies in the Americas learned that France now controlled Spain, poor Indians, free blacks, and people of mixed race joined forces with creole rebels who were motivated by a pent-up desire to run things themselves after years of taking orders from the peninsulars.

Several territories declared their independence from French-controlled Spain from 1810 to 1814, most notably New Spain (which included Central America and the southwestern quadrant of North America). Most of these early independence movements vowed to chart their own course only until King Ferdinand was restored to the throne. Historians agree, however, that these self-proclaimed patriots were not genuinely allegiant to the Spanish Crown. They just wanted to blunt opposition to their actions from the colonies' powerful peninsulars, who remained staunch "royalists"—supporters of King Ferdinand and the Spanish government.

The rebels made their desire for true independence clear after Napoleon was defeated and King Ferdinand returned to the throne in 1814. Ferdinand refused to accept the loss of Spanish America. He sent armies to the Americas to keep the Spanish flag flying over the colonies. But the rebels fought back with grit and determination, led by inspirational figures like Miguel Hidalgo y Costilla, who helped spark the successful revolution in Mexico; José de San Martin, who led triumphant revolutions against Spanish rule in Argentina, Chile, and Peru; and Simón Bolivar, a wealthy Venezuelan creole who helped bring independence to half a dozen Latin American countries. By 1826 the only remnants of Spain's New World empire that remained in Spanish hands were the islands of Cuba and Puerto Rico.

The patriots who took part in these drives for independence from Spanish rule took great satisfaction in their accomplishments. The disintegration of Spanish America into independent nations was accompanied by great pain and sorrow, though. "The conflicts differed from country to country, yet everywhere the human toll was immense," wrote journalist Juan Gonzalez. "The mammoth size of the colonies made for an epic, disordered, and bloody canvas. Mexico's independence wars, for instance, began in 1810.... By the time the wars ended in 1821, more than 600,000 were dead, 10 percent of the country's population."[9]

Spain lost the territory of Florida during this period as well, though not by revolution. Florida had been a jewel in Spain's colonial crown since the mid-sixteenth century, but by the early 1800s Spain had become so weak that it could no longer defend its claim on the land. When "Anglo" settlers—white people who spoke English—began pouring into Florida from the United States in the early 1800s, the lightly manned Spanish garrisons in the region could not stop them. Spain reluctantly decided to sell the land before it was taken away. In 1819 Spain and the United States signed the Adams-Onís Treaty, which transferred ownership of Florida to the Americans. In exchange, the United States agreed to an international boundary that placed another disputed territory—Texas—within the Spanish province of Mexico. Within a few years, though, Mexico had gained its independence, leaving Spain with nothing to show for its trade.

Mexico Confronts an Emerging American Empire

The new Latin American nations that arose out of the old Spanish colonies were economically weak and politically unstable. Mexico was no exception, even though it occupied an impressive amount of space on continental maps

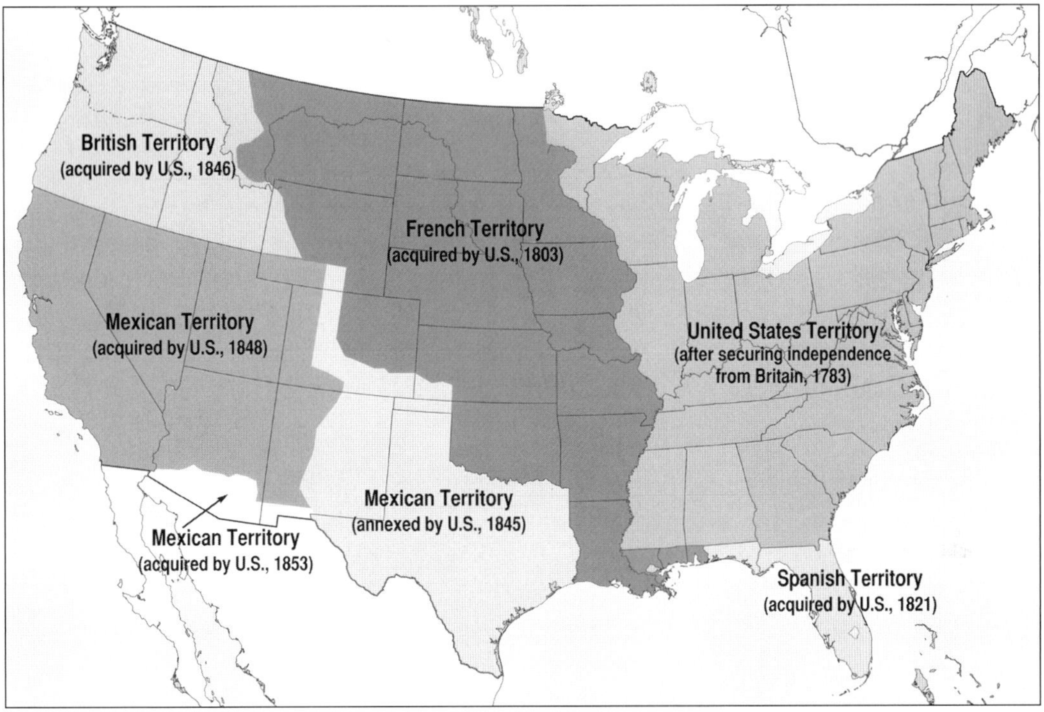

Territorial expansion of the United States in the nineteenth century.

of the 1820s and 1830s. Its territory extended from the Yucatan Peninsula in the south to the northern border of what is now the state of California. It also sprawled from the shores of the Pacific Ocean deep into the continent's western interior, to include formerly Spanish-held lands in modern-day Colorado, Oklahoma, and Texas.

Mexico had the misfortune of being born at the same time that the United States was actively seeking to expand its land holdings. Nineteenth-century Americans were developing a fervent belief in "manifest destiny"—the idea that God had *chosen* the United States to settle and rule the North American continent. When land-hungry American lawmakers, railroad owners, land speculators, bankers, merchants, and farmers looked to Mexico's northern territories, they saw a rich land full of virgin timber, fertile soil, abundant wildlife, and mighty rivers that rightfully belonged to them. These same Anglos viewed the Native American tribes and Mexicans who already lived in the region as obstacles to their empire-building dreams. They believed that, one way or another,

The First Cowboys of the West

Engraving of Mexican *vaqueros* (cowboys) tending the livestock of a wealthy hacienda owner in nineteenth-century California.

When Spaniards first came to the New World, they introduced horses and domesticated cattle to the Americas as well. By the nineteenth

the Mexicans and Indians would have to give way to America's need for territorial expansion.

The Mexicans recognized that the Anglos posed a potential threat. Yet Mexican authorities did not have the military power to turn back Anglo settlers. With this in mind, they tried to get along with their American neighbors. In 1821, for instance, they agreed to let an American named Stephen F. Austin carry century, one or both of these animals had become integral to the economies and cultures of whites, numerous Native American tribes, and the Spanish-speaking peoples of Mexico and the American Southwest. The horsemen who came from the Spanish tradition were known as *vaqueros,* and they were recognized in Texas, California, and everywhere in between for their skill in capturing wild mustangs and managing cattle herds. Most of these vaqueros—or cowboys—were mestizos or mulattoes.

After Mexico lost its northern territories to the United States in the mid-1800s, American ranchers converted these new properties into vast rangelands for cattle. The beef industry expanded rapidly in the second half of the nineteenth century thanks to the growth of the railroads and immigration-fueled increases in the overall U.S. population. But this success also stemmed from the talents of the Mexican vaqueros, who were recognized as masters of the saddle. "All of the [American] skills, traditions, and ways of working with cattle are very much rooted in the Mexican vaquero," western historian Kendall Nelson told *National Geographic News.* "Anglo cowboys copied virtually all the culture of the range from them," confirmed scholar Juan Gonzales. "Yet the cowboy myth in popular folklore, the one Hollywood has propagated around the world, is of a lone white Anglo sitting tall in the saddle, with Mexicans of the Old West invariably portrayed either as bandits or doltish peasants riding donkeys."

Sources:

Gonzalez, Juan. *Harvest of Empire: A History of Latinos in America.* New York: Viking, 2000, pp. 44-45.

Haeber, Jonathan. "Vaqueros: The First Cowboys of the Open Range." *National Geographic News,* August 15, 2003. Retrieved from news.nationalgeographic.com/news/2003/08/0814_030815_cowboys.html.

out a settlement plan in Texas that had originally been approved by the Spanish Crown. The only conditions of settlement were that Austin and the 300 Anglo farming families he brought with him had to swear allegiance to Mexico and convert to Catholicism.

Austin and his group subsequently established the township of San Filepe, which became so prosperous that it attracted a huge influx of new Anglo settlers into the territory. This development greatly alarmed the Mexican authorities, who worried that their hospitality had backfired. "Where others send invading armies," warned Mexican secretary of state Lucas Alaman, "[the Americans] send their colonists.... Texas will be lost for this Republic if adequate measures to save it are not taken."[10]

The War for Texas

Mexico rolled out several policies designed to shut off the flow of Anglo settlers into Texas. In the late 1820s the government outlawed slavery across all of Mexico, including Texas. Mexican officials hoped that this measure would make the territory less attractive to the white Americans, many of whom kept slaves. Mexico also raised taxes on Anglo settlers, and in 1830 it passed a law that prohibited immigration from the United States to Texas. The Anglo settlers, though, ignored all of these laws and continued to pour into Texas. By 1834 Anglos outnumbered Spanish-speaking Mexicans in the territory by better than four to one.

In 1836 Austin and his fellow Anglos declared Texan independence from Mexico. This defiance received a stern response from General Antonio López de Santa Anna, who at that time sat atop Mexico's unstable political scene. Santa Anna took personal command of an army charged with crushing the rebellion and bringing Texas back under Mexican control. On March 6, 1836, Santa Anna's troops famously massacred a group of about 200 Texan rebels—including famous frontiersmen Davy Crockett and Jim Bowie—at the Battle of the Alamo in San Antonio. Less than two months later, though, Santa Anna suffered a crushing defeat at the hands of Sam Houston at the Battle of San Jacinto.

The Texan triumph at San Jacinto paved the way for Anglos in Texas to achieve independence in 1836. The Texans immediately began lobbying for membership in the United States, and in 1845 the U.S. Congress officially annexed the territory. This development outraged Mexico, which had never accepted the legality of Texas's claim of independence. With all diplomatic options exhausted, the two nations finally went to war in May 1846.

A New Flag Flies Over California and the Southwest

The Mexican-American War lasted for two long years, during which time U.S. military forces invaded California and other large swaths of Mexico's northern territories. The American offensive was a ruthless and destructive one that took a heavy toll on Mexican soldiers and civilians alike. "The [American]

In March 1836 Mexican troops overwhelmed rebellious American settlers at the famous Battle of the Alamo.

artillery bombardments were terrible everywhere," wrote Shorris. "Hospitals and churches were destroyed; women and children died more often than soldiers. The destruction of captured territory had no military value, yet town after town was left ruined, blown apart and burned to the ground."[11]

The decisive campaign of the war came in mid-1847, when U.S. general Winfield Scott led a military invasion deep into the heart of Mexico. In September 1847 Scott's forces marched into Mexico City, the nation's capital. The American occupation of Mexico City was a stunning setback for Mexico. Santa Anna and other Mexican commanders tried to keep military operations going against the American invaders even after the loss of Mexico City, but their efforts failed. Most Mexicans laid down their arms in recognition that they were simply no match for the American military machine moving through their countryside. As Scott consolidated his position across Mexico, Mexican officials signaled their willingness to agree to peace on America's terms.

The Mexican-American War, wrote Civil War general and U.S. president Ulysses S. Grant, was "one of the most unjust ever waged by a stronger against a weaker nation."

The Mexican-American War came to a close with the signing of the Treaty of Guadalupe Hidalgo on February 2, 1848. The terms of the treaty were extremely one-sided. The United States gave Mexico $18.25 million for war damages and agreed to pay an additional $3.25 million in debt owed by the Mexican government to American citizens. In exchange, Mexico handed over possession of all its northern territories—roughly half of the land mass of the entire country—to the United States. This 525,000-square-mile bloc of land included all or most of the present-day states of Arizona, California, Colorado, Nevada, New Mexico, Texas, and Utah, as well as parts of Oklahoma, Kansas, and Wyoming (in 1853 the United States bought another 30,000 square miles of Mexican territory through the Gadsden Purchase; this acquisition boosted Arizona and New Mexico to their present borders).

Many Americans praised the acquisition of all this land as a fulfillment of the nation's Manifest Destiny. Other Americans, however, were not so proud of the Mexican-American War. Ulysses S. Grant, who served as a general in both the Mexican-American War and the Civil War before becoming the eighteenth president of the United States, wrote in his memoirs that the war against Mexico was "one of the most unjust ever waged by a stronger against a weaker nation."[12]

The California Gold Rush

To Mexican families who had been born and raised in California and other parts of the Southwest, the transfer of ownership of their homeland to the United States was profoundly disorienting. Seemingly in the blink of an eye, these

An idyllic Currier & Ives representation of the life of a gold miner in California in the late 1800s.

Spanish-speaking Catholics found themselves living in a world that was controlled by English-speaking Protestants.

The Mexicans' plight worsened in 1849, when thousands of prospectors descended on California in search of gold. This California Gold Rush, as it came to be known, was sparked by the 1848 discovery of gold at Sutter's Mill, a small sawmill on the banks of California's American River. Within a year of that gold strike, the territory's non-Indian population had jumped from 20,000 to 100,000, far outnumbering the 13,000 or so *Californios*—Catholics of Spanish descent who made their homes in California.

Once the gold fever died down, many of the Anglo immigrants decided to support themselves by establishing farms and ranches on the large haciendas owned by the Californios. When the Californios objected to these blatant invasions of their property, they received little support from the U.S. legal system. Instead, Anglo-controlled courts and legislatures worked together to separate the Californios from lands that had been passed down over multiple generations (See "Anglo Squatters Swarm Mexican-Owned Haciendas in California," p. 153).

Ordinary Mexicans, meanwhile, experienced discrimination from Anglos in their quest for jobs and other economic opportunities in the West. "The victory of the Anglos was quick and cruel," wrote Shorris. "In less than a quarter-century, the people who had taken the Pacific coast from the Native Americans lost it to the Anglo-Americans."[13]

Notes:

[1] Shorris, Earl. *Latinos: A Biography of the People.* New York: W. W. Norton, 1992, p. 21.
[2] Quoted in Días del Castillo, Bernal. *The Conquest of New Spain.* London: Penguin Books, 1963, p. 235.
[3] Quoted in *General History of the Things of New Spain,* translated by Arthur J. O. Anderson and Charles E. Dibble. In *PBS: Conquistadores* [online], 2000. Retrieved from www.pbs.org/conquistadores/cortes/cortes_g01.html.
[4] Bernand, Carmen. *The Incas: People of the Sun.* New York: Henry N. Abrams, 1994, p. 159.
[5] Shorris, p. 23.
[6] Shorris, p. 17.
[7] Klein, Herbert S. *African Slavery in Latin America and the Caribbean.* Oxford, UK: Oxford University Press, 1986, pp. 22.
[8] Quoted in "Chapter 4: How Contact Changed the New World." *When Worlds Collide: The Untold Story of the Americas After Columbus,* 2010. http://www.pbs.org/kcet/when-worlds-collide/story/story-chapter-4.html.
[9] Gonzalez, Juan. *Harvest of Empire: A History of Latinos in America.* New York: Viking, 2000, p. 32.
[10] Quoted in Gonzalez, p. 41.
[11] Shorris, p. 39.
[12] Grant, Ulysses S. *Personal Memoirs of U. S. Grant.* New York: Charles L. Webster, 1885, p. 22.
[13] Shorris, pp. 32-33.

Chapter Two

RISING TENSIONS IN CALIFORNIA

> The slogan has gone out over the city [of Los Angeles] and is being adhered to—"Employ no Mexican while a white man is unemployed.... It is a question of pigment, not a question of citizenship or right."[1]
>
> —George Clements, agriculture manager of the Los Angeles Chamber of Commerce, 1930

By the closing years of the nineteenth century, the United States appeared poised to become the world's next great economic, political, and military power. The country possessed all the ingredients necessary to rise to the top ranks of nations, from industrial might and money for investment to a vast pool of tough, ambitious, and inexpensive immigrant workers that was being replenished every year from overseas. All of these assets enabled the United States to rapidly develop its resource-rich western lands, most of which had been forcibly taken from Mexico in the mid-1800s.

Meanwhile, Spain's once-formidable colonial empire had been greatly reduced. Most of its possessions in the Americas had been lost to native independence movements in the early 1800s, and by the end of that century it had reason to worry that its remaining colonial holdings might slip out of its grasp as well. Both the Philippine Islands (in the southwestern Pacific Ocean) and Cuba (in the Caribbean) were rocked by revolutionary independence movements in the late 1800s. The Spanish Crown tried to smother these revolts through a combination of political reforms and military actions. In April 1898, though, the United States stepped in and used its superior military power to pry Cuba, the Philippines, Puerto Rico, and Guam out of Spain's grip.

A Cuban laborer cutting cane on one of the country's vast U.S.-owned sugar cane plantations.

By the time the so-called Spanish-American War had concluded in December 1898—a mere eight months after it began—the Philippines, Puerto Rico, and Guam had become U.S. possessions. Cuba, meanwhile, became a nominally independent nation. In reality, though, the Cubans were independent in name only. The United States arranged Cuba's political and economic affairs in ways that gave the Americans heavy influence over the island nation for the next half-century.

An Unequal Relationship

Cuba was not the only nation that fell under the economic and political spell of the United States. During the early 1900s it became clear that virtually all of the peoples that had once sworn allegiance to the Spanish Crown were now controlled to one degree or another by the United States. American influence stemmed from its corporations, which gained control over mining, gas, railroads, agriculture, and other key industries throughout the Americas. Working hand in hand with the U.S. government, these businesses were able to apply enormous political pressure on any foreign leaders or native workers who threatened their profits. The most powerful of these corporations was probably the United Fruit Company, which held vast fruit-growing plantations throughout Central America and the Caribbean. "More than any other U.S. company, United Fruit became the twentieth-century symbol of U.S. imperialism," wrote journalist Juan Gonzalez. "It would evolve into a corporate octopus, controlling the livelihoods of hundreds of thousands and toppling governments at will."[2]

In cases where political or economic pressure was not enough to subdue opposition, the U.S. government deployed soldiers to protect American commercial interests in Mexico, Central America, and the Caribbean. Nicaragua, for instance, was under almost continuous U.S. military occupation from 1912 to 1933, while U.S. Marines controlled the Dominican Republic from 1916 to 1924.

American officials, corporate executives, and military leaders defended these military actions as necessary to preserve the stability of foreign nations and the health of American businesses operating in those countries. Critics, though, said that these "banana wars"—so named because bananas were one of the main products grown by U.S. companies in several of these countries—showed that America was not treating its foreign neighbors in accordance with its stated ideals of freedom and justice. They pointed out that while U.S. companies operating in Mexico, Central America, and the Caribbean were pulling great riches out of those regions, most natives of those countries remained poor, uneducated, and politically powerless.

Refugees from Poverty and War

In the early 1900s living conditions in Mexico became so bad that thousands of Mexicans fled across the northern border to the United States in search of a better life. This exodus from Mexico started around 1906, when the Mexican economy went into a deep depression. It accelerated in 1910, when Mexico fell into civil war. The Mexican Revolution of 1910 lasted for a full ten years, during which time life became even harder for the Indians, mestizos, mulattoes, and other racially mixed groups that made up Mexico's large peasant class. Some Mexicans took up arms for one side or another, but an estimated 250,000 others fled to the United States to escape the violence and turmoil in their homeland.

The primary destinations of the Mexican refugees were the border states of Texas and California, where they found work in orchards, fields, canneries, and other factories. Some refugees, though, dispersed as far as the factories of the upper Midwest, which faced labor shortages after America entered World War I in 1917. Almost all of this immigration took place legally, with the new arrivals paying a nickel apiece for visas (a visa is a legal document confirming that the holder is allowed to stay and work in the country for a certain period of time). "The vast majority were here legally, because it was so easy to enter legally,"[3] said scholar Kevin Johnson.

A few of the Mexican immigrants to the United States during the 1910s and 1920s were wealthy and educated men and women of Spanish descent. Most of them settled among the Californios that had managed to preserve ownership of at least a portion of their once-great haciendas. The vast majority of Mexicans who came to America, though, had little choice but to move into slums or seasonal shacks that California's big farms and orchards maintained for their field hands. "They had no skills, little or no education, and they could not speak English," summarized historian Earl Shorris. "They were forced to work for the lowest wages in the worst jobs. Nevertheless, it was better than life in Mexico during a civil war in which the population of the country was decimated."[4]

Life in America was also eased by the establishment of entire neighborhoods of Spanish-speaking families. These neighborhoods, known as *barrios*, gave many Mexican families a sense of belonging and solidarity within the strange and often-unfriendly land in which they found themselves. "For the Mexicans the barrio was a colony of refugees," recalled author Ernesto Galarza, who moved with his family to Sacramento, California, in 1913, when he was eight years old. "We came to know families from Chihuahua, Sonora, Jalisco, and Durango. Some had come to the United States even before the revolution, living in Texas before migrating to California. Like ourselves, our Mexican neighbors had come this far moving step by step, working and waiting, as if they were feeling their way up a ladder.... [The barrio] kept filling with newcomers who found families who took in boarders, in basements, alleys, shanties, run-down rooming houses, and flop joints where they could live."[5]

Even within the barrio, though, there existed different cultural traditions. *Chicanos,* for instance, were people born and raised in Mexico. They came to America armed with a deep affection for and knowledge of the language and traditions of their homeland. *Pochos,* on the other hand, were people of Mexican heritage who had actually been born in California or other parts of America, and who frequently had a better command of English than Spanish. These Mexican Americans, as they would come to see themselves, were legally recognized as full citizens of the United States because they had been born on American soil. "The *chicanos* and the *pochos* had certain feelings about one another," wrote Galarza. "Concerning the *pochos,* the *chicanos* suspected that they considered themselves too good for the barrio but were not, for some reason, good enough for the Americans. Toward the *chicanos,* the *pochos* acted superior, amused at our confusions but not especially interested in explaining them to us.... Turning *pocho* was a half step toward turning American. And America was all around us, in and out of the barrio."[6]

Whatever their differences, however, the native-born Mexican Americans and the Mexican immigrants frequently worked together to improve the com-

Mexican children and families in southern Texas after fleeing the turmoil of the Mexican Revolution.

munities in which they both lived. They also toiled side by side in the mines, factories, railroad yards, and fields of the West. By the 1920s, in fact, probably three out of four of California's 200,000 farm workers were either Mexicans or Mexican Americans. They also were a vital, if unappreciated, driver of economic growth in Los Angeles, San Diego, Sacramento, and other fast-growing cities up and down the coast. "Many businesses in southern California relied heavily on trade between Mexico and the United States," noted historian Eduardo Obregón Pagán. "The city of Los Angeles itself was dependent on tax revenues from Mexican vendors and businesses or on businesses that thrived on the patronage of Mexicans and Mexican Americans."[7]

Boom Years in California

Several cities in California experienced rapid population growth and economic development in the 1910s and 1920s, but none could match Los Ange-

Portrait of a Mexican-American grocery store owner and his family in Los Angeles, c. 1924.

les's explosive expansion. Boosted by city planners who were both imaginative and ruthless in buying up regional water rights and land, Los Angeles grew by leaps and bounds. By 1932, in fact, the city covered about 450 square miles of coastal southern California.

A major hub of industrial agriculture, manufacturing, and transportation, Los Angeles also became a shaper of American popular culture. The city's Hollywood district emerged as the home of America's fast-growing motion picture industry in the 1920s and 1930s. Meanwhile, the city's jazz, blues, and swing clubs ranked among the most famous in the country. Legendary performers like Jelly Roll Morton, Kid Ory, Lionel Hampton, and Benny Goodman played these exciting new forms of music to raucous crowds filled with young dancers of every race and background. "There were a lot of blacks, a lot of Mexicans" at the city's clubs, theaters, and concert halls, recalled Arthur Arenas, a Mexican-American resident of Los Angeles. "They would go to their theaters that they like, you know? And if you liked big band music ... you had your choice, because it was packed. Everybody would go downtown. You'd see every color and creed downtown."[8]

As the economic lights of Los Angeles grew brighter and brighter, real estate developers also emphasized southern California's beautiful weather and scenery. Their descriptions of the "Golden State" attracted legions of affluent white Americans from all across the country. Once they arrived in Los Angeles, many of these new "Angelenos" (Los Angeles residents) settled in white-only neighborhoods and communities.

Strong feelings of racism and nativism—favoritism toward native inhabitants of a land and hostility toward immigrants—were common in these communities (see "Examples of Anti-Mexican Discrimination in 1930s America," p. 156). The whites who controlled Los Angeles's political and economic levers were happy to make use of the cheap labor that Mexican, Japanese, Filipino, and African-American workers provided. In addition, California's historical links to Spain became a centerpiece of the city's fast-growing tourism industry. The city's white officials and boosters restored the old Spanish missions that dotted the region and marketed them as a romantic slice of history. They also incorporated Mexican and Spanish artistic and architectural influences into new buildings on the city's university campuses and downtown business district. "Entrepreneurs needed enough cultural difference in Los Angeles and enough exoticism to sell the myth of Old Mexico to tourists who wished to sample a bit of Mexico but stay north of the border," said Pagán. "Los Angeles offered a safer, more sanitized version of Mexico."[9]

Many white Angelenos worried, though, that Los Angeles's rapid growth was drawing *too many* minority workers and families. They saw the growing racial diversity in Los Angeles (and the wider state) as a threat to their Protestant culture and way of life, not as a resource that could make their communities even stronger. These attitudes allowed white supremacist organizations like the Ku Klux Klan to flourish in Los Angeles and other California cities and towns during the 1920s and 1930s.

Battered by the Great Depression

Daily life in Los Angeles and other parts of California and the wider West became much more difficult for Mexican and Mexican-American families in the

An aerial view of Hollywood's Grauman's Chinese Theatre, one of the most famous movie theatres in America, on its opening night in 1927.

1930s, when the Great Depression rocked the foundations of American society. This terrible economic slump, which began in late 1929 and lasted until 1939, triggered frightening levels of poverty and unemployment in America and around the world. In the United States this downturn was made even worse by the onset of the Dust Bowl, a series of mid-1930s droughts and dust storms that brought economic and environmental devastation to farmers in the Great Plains states. Many of these farmers abandoned their homes and fled westward, hoping to find better living and working conditions in the fields and orchards of California.

When the Great Depression hit, the competition for jobs in California and elsewhere quickly intensified. Desperate white workers claimed that Mexican immigrants, African Americans, and other minorities were occupying jobs that should go to white people. Many white business owners and public officials shared this belief. Others saw the economic turmoil of the Great Depression as an opportunity to derail a growing movement among Mexican, Mexican-American, and other nonwhite workers to band together and protest the meager wages and shoddy housing provided by white farm and cannery owners.

Finally, some white officials, civic leaders, and workers complained that people of Mexican heritage were receiving too much of the relief funding and programs that local, state, and federal government agencies provided to struggling Americans during the Depression years. This line of attack put Mexican and Mexican-American families in a no-win situation. If they were able to keep their jobs, then critics complained that they were depriving more deserving white workers of employment. But if they lost their jobs—oftentimes simply for being of Mexican descent—then whites criticized them for relying on welfare or other forms of public assistance.

Repatriation Program of the 1930s

By 1930 the U.S. Census counted 1.42 million people of Mexican ancestry in the United States, including more than 800,000 who had been born in America and were thus U.S. citizens. People of Mexican heritage thus accounted for only a little more than one percent of the total U.S. population of 123 million. In some western cities, though, people of Mexican descent accounted for a considerably higher percentage of the overall population. In 1930 Los Angeles, for example, the U.S. Census indicated that roughly one out of twelve residents fit into the category of "Mexican."

That same year, government officials in California and around the country decided that these numbers were too high. Prodded by white economic anxiety and strong currents of nativism, they approved measures to reduce the number of Mexicans and Mexican Americans living and working in the United States. One part of this strategy involved choking off the flow of legal immigration into the United States from Mexico. The centerpiece of this campaign, though, was a "repatriation" (deportation) program designed to scour American cities of many of their Mexican and Mexican-American residents. These repatriation policies were formed by local and state governments with the approval of President Herbert Hoover's administration and carried out all across the country in the early 1930s.

The campaigns were particularly harsh and wide-reaching in Los Angeles and other California cities with large Hispanic populations (see "Depression-Era Los Angeles Targets Mexicans for Repatriation," p. 161). "No other locality matched the county of Los Angeles in its ambitious efforts to rid itself of the Mexican immigrant during the depression years," wrote historian Abraham Hoffman. "By defining people along cultural instead of national lines, county officials deprived American children of Mexican descent of rights guaranteed them by the Constitution."[10] The exact number of people of Mexican heritage who were pressured to leave or actually evicted from Los Angeles as a result of the city's repatriation program is unknown, but some historians believe that the total reached about 35,000—approximately one-third of the city's Hispanic population.[11]

"Thousands upon thousands of Mexican aliens [have been] literally scared out of Southern California," wrote Walter Carr, Los Angeles district director of immigration.

Scholars disagree about the total national scale of the repatriation programs. Some historians believe that as many as one million people of Mexican descent were directly affected by the campaign. Others place the number of repatriated people of Hispanic heritage at 400,000-500,000. Whatever the total number of people affected, the individuals and families ensnared in this campaign found their lives turned upside down with terrifying swiftness. "Most of the deportations were done by force," stated California state senator Joe Dunn, who convinced the state to pass a bill formally apologizing for its deportation program in 2006, more than seventy years later. "Most of the deportees that were shipped to Mexico did not speak the [Spanish] language. And they were not only thrown out of their country of birth, the United States, they were foreigners in the new land that they were shipped to, that being Mexico."[12]

Other people of Mexican heritage fled the United States in order to avoid the prospect of seeing their loved ones rounded up against their will (some victims of the deportation crusade were even taken into custody at gunpoint). "Thousands upon thousands of Mexican aliens [have been] literally scared out of Southern California,"[13] wrote Walter Carr, the Los Angeles district director of immigration, in 1931.

The government of Mexico tried to assist these new arrivals, which the Mexican people referred to as *repatriados*. Most of these financial aid and land ownership programs were inadequate, though. Thousands of families—including many that were entirely or partly composed of American citizens—never recovered from the emotional, cultural, and financial disruption of their deportation from the United States. "Families caught by the repatriation dragnet struggled to understand what was happening to them," wrote historians Francisco E. Balderrama and Raymond Rodríguez. "Why were they being singled out? Why were none of the other racial and ethnic groups being expelled to their ancestral lands? Children, especially teenagers, found it impossible to believe ... that the land of their birth was callously dispatching them to a foreign country.... When asked if he wanted to go back to Mexico, one ten-year-old youngster responded candidly, No! It is like being sent to Mars."[14]

Many of the repatriados remained stranded in Mexico, unable to make a legal return to the United States, because they had been deported before they could secure their birth certificates or other proof of U.S. citizenship. Mexican Americans described this situation as an outrage, and some white liberals joined them in criticizing such blatant disregard for constitutional rights.

Advocates of repatriation generally ignored these complaints, but one prominent supporter of the program casually acknowledged that the criticisms were valid. "No child could return, even though born in America, unless he had documentary evidence and his birth certificate and was able to substantiate this, the burden of proof being placed entirely on the individual," said Los Angeles official George Clements, one of the most outspoken champions of that city's deportation program. "This means that something like 60% of these children are American citizens without very much hope of ever coming back into the United States."[15]

America Invites Mexican Workers to Return

In 1942 the United States abruptly changed its attitude about Mexican workers yet again. Only a decade after launching a repatriation program that had either forced or intimidated hundreds of thousands of legal Mexican immigrants and Mexican-American citizens into leaving the United States, federal authorities rolled out a new program that actually *encouraged* workers from Mexico to come to America. It was, according to U.S. scholar Nancy Brown Diggs, one of the clearest historical examples of how America "has waxed and waned in its reception of those coming from Mexico, welcoming immigrants when we need them, rejecting them when we do not."[16]

The Bracero Program, also known as the Emergency Labor Program, had been approved by Congress shortly after the United States entered World War II

The institution of America's Bracero program in 1942 brought millions of Mexican laborers to the United States.

in December 1941. It was designed to use Mexicans to replenish the work forces of big farming outfits in California and other parts of the West. These agribusinesses were losing large numbers of employees to the military and to the industrial factories that were churning out rifles, jeeps, airplanes, and other wartime supplies for the U.S. military. They accurately saw Mexico as a resource that could be tapped for large numbers of low-cost workers.

As expected, large numbers of impoverished Mexicans leaped at the chance to go to the United States. This *Bracero*, or "guest worker," program ultimately brought four to five million Mexican workers to the United States from 1942 to 1964, when the program ended. Even Mexicans and Mexican Americans who had been chased out of the country back in the 1930s signed up for the program.

The majority of Braceros, though, were Mexicans who were leaving their native country for the first time. "I really needed to go because I had a son that was ill, and I needed the money for his surgery," remembered one Bracero contract worker who made the journey with a friend. "When we crossed the border at Ciudad Juárez, our hearts pounded wildly. We were afraid because we were in a totally strange country, and I had never really done any other kind of work but mine [as a driver in the Mexican Army].... It was a long way from Ciudad Juárez to California. During the trip we entertained ourselves by counting the wagons on the trains that were going by with military equipment and personnel on their way to Europe. Sometimes the soldiers would wave at us and we waved back. The trains passed really close to each other and sometimes the American soldiers would even give us a cigarette."[17]

The Bracero Program had actually been put together in cooperation with the Mexican government, which insisted that all braceros receive a guaranteed minimum wage and decent housing from their agricultural employers. However, workers enrolled in the program were restricted to agricultural jobs. Legally forbidden from pursuing higher-paying jobs in manufacturing or other industries, the braceros were at the mercy of the American growers who employed them.

Unfortunately for the braceros who made the trip north, many of the California farm owners did not treat them fairly. "Bracero workers complained of violations of wage agreements, substandard living quarters, exorbitant charges for food and clothing, and racist discrimination," noted one history of Hispanics in California. "The bracero camps became a special kind of Mexican community in many rural areas of the Southwest. As a camp they were segregated from whites and even from the Mexican-American sections of town. Braceros lived in extreme poverty and worked in dangerous conditions. When they ventured outside the camps on weekends they frequently were the victims of racially inspired beatings and robberies."[18]

Meanwhile, the fresh influx of Mexican immigrants into the American Southwest triggered another wave of contradictory reactions from white residents. On the one hand, white anxiety about increased competition for jobs rose once again. Some whites also expressed fears that the Mexicans would bring higher levels of crime, poverty, inner-city overcrowding, and an overall erosion of white Anglo culture. These concerns led many whites to support "Americanization" campaigns. These programs were designed to scrub Mexicans and other immigrants of their cultural history and convince them to accept "American"—meaning white Anglo—values and customs, including the English language.

Many white business owners and civic leaders, though, recognized the economic value of their Mexican and Mexican-American communities. In addition, white liberals joined Mexican and Mexican-American leaders in strongly defending both the proud cultural heritage and the basic humanity of Hispanics in California and elsewhere. These voices insisted that Hispanics and other minorities could fully embrace the rights and responsibilities of American citizenship without forsaking their ethnic heritage or cultural traditions.

Mass Internment of Japanese Americans during World War II

In late 1941 and 1942 the debate over the role and influence of Mexicans and other minorities in California temporarily faded in intensity. Instead, white residents of Los Angeles and other coastal cities focused their attention on Japanese Americans. This shift was a direct result of the December 7, 1941, sneak attack by Japanese fighter planes on the U.S. Navy base at Pearl Harbor in Hawaii. The devastating assault not only convinced the United States to enter World War II, it also cast a cloud of suspicion over people of Japanese descent living in America.

In the aftermath of the attack, the American public, news media, and prominent civic organizations like the American Legion and the Chamber of Commerce all demanded that the U.S. government take steps to protect the country from the potentially traitorous Japanese living in their midst. "I am for immediate removal of every Japanese on the West Coast to a point deep in the interior," declared syndicated columnist Henry McLemore of the *San Francisco Examiner.* "I don't mean a nice part of the interior either.... Let us have no

Japanese-American evacuees in Los Angeles in 1942 preparing to board a train that will take them to internment camps for the duration of World War II.

patience with the enemy or with anyone whose veins carry his blood.... Personally, I hate the Japanese, and that goes for all of them."[19]

The administration of President Franklin D. Roosevelt responded by ordering the imprisonment of the entire Japanese-American population, as well as Japanese citizens legally working in the United States. Roosevelt's Executive Order 9066, which he signed on February 19, 1942, ultimately resulted in the forced relocation of about 120,000 people of Japanese ancestry into "internment camps" scattered across the American West. About two-thirds of the victims of this action were U.S.-born American citizens. Nonetheless, they were forced to hurriedly sell their homes and belongings. Everything they could not sell or give away they had to abandon.

Supporters of Japanese internment argued that it was necessary to protect the United States from acts of sabotage by spies. After the war concluded and the Japanese-American prisoners were released, however, many Americans expressed shame about the episode, which trampled so blatantly on the civil rights of thousands of American citizens. In 1982 a special government investigation conducted by the Commission on Wartime Relocation and Internment of Civilians reported that America's World War II internment policies were "motivated largely by racial prejudice, wartime hysteria, and a failure of political leadership."[20]

For Hispanics, the anti-Japanese sentiment that saturated Los Angeles and other West Coast cities in early 1942 briefly took them out of the racial spotlight. Whites who were anxious about the growing numbers of nonwhite races in their midst expressed far more concern about Japanese traitors than Mexican laborers. Soon enough, though, it became clear that Japanese Americans were not the only minority group that would attract heightened scrutiny from whites in wartime California.

Notes:

[1] Koch, Wendy. "U.S. Urged to Apologize for 1930s Deportations." *USA Today,* April 5, 2006. Retrieved from www.usatoday.com/news/nation/2006-04-04-1930s-deportees-cover_x.htm.

[2] Gonzalez, Juan. *Harvest of Empire: A History of Latinos in America.* New York: Viking, 2000, p. 57.

[3] Quoted in Koch.

[4] Shorris, Earl. *Latinos: A Biography of the People.* New York: W. W. Norton, 1992, p. 42.

[5] Galarza, Ernesto. Excerpt from *Barrio Boy.* In Heide, Rick, ed. *Under the Fifth Sun: Latino Literature from California.* Berkeley, CA: Heyday Books/Santa Clara University, 2002, p. 415.

[6] Galarza, p. 421.

[7] Pagán, Eduardo Obregón. *Murder at the Sleepy Lagoon: Zoot Suits, Race, and Riot in Wartime L.A.* Chapel Hill: University of North Carolina Press, 2003, p. 26.

[8] Quoted in "Zoot Suit Culture." *PBS American Experience: The Zoot Suit Riots,* 2001. Retrieved from www.pbs.org/wgbh/amex/zoot/eng_sfeature/sf_zoot_text.html.

[9] Pagán, p, 27.

[10] Hoffman, Abraham. *Unwanted Mexican Americans in the Great Depression: Repatriation Pressures, 1929-1939.* Tucson: University of Arizona Press, 1974, p. 3.

[11] Meier, Matt, and Feliciano Rivera. *The Chicanos: A History of Mexican Americans.* New York: Hill and Wang, 1972, p. 161.

[12] Quoted in "Remembering California's 'Repatriation Program.'" *National Public Radio (NPR): All Things Considered,* January 2, 2006. Retrieved from www.npr.org/templates/story/story.php?storyId=5079627.

[13] Quoted in Koch.

[14] Balderrama, Francisco E., and Raymond Rodríguez. *Decade of Betrayal: Mexican Repatriation in the 1930s.* Albuquerque: University of New Mexico Press, 2006, p. 266.

[15] Quoted in Hoffman, p. 95.

[16] Diggs, Nancy Brown. *Hidden in the Heartland: The New Wave of Immigrants and the Challenge to America.* East Lansing: Michigan State University Press, 2011.

[17] "A Bracero Remembers." In Chapter 8: World War II and the Emerging Civil Rights Struggle, *San Diego Mexican and Chicano History* Web site. Retrieved from aztlan.sdsu.edu/chicanohistory/chapter08/c08s07.html.

[18] "Who Were the Braceros and What Was Their Experience?" In Chapter 8: World War II and the Emerging Civil Rights Struggle, *San Diego Mexican and Chicano History* Web site. Retrieved from aztlan.sdsu.edu/chicanohistory/chapter08/c08s06.html.

[19] Quoted in Spickard, Paul R. *Almost All Aliens: Immigration, Race, and Colonialism in American History and Identity.* New York: Taylor & Francis, 2009, p. 319.

[20] Quoted in "Internment History." *Children of the Camps*, 1999. Retrieved from www.pbs.org/childofcamp/history/index.html.

Chapter Three

A CITY ON EDGE

> We're tired of being told we can't go to this show or this dance hall because we're Mexican or that we better not be seen on the beach front, or that we can't wear draped pants or have our hair cut the way we want to.[1]
>
> —A Mexican-American zoot suiter in World War II-era Los Angeles

After the U.S. government decided to imprison its Japanese-American population in internment camps for the duration of World War II, white Californians turned their anxious gaze toward the growing numbers of Mexican Americans and Mexican immigrants in their midst. The bombing of Pearl Harbor had brought to the surface long-simmering white anxieties about nonwhites living and working in the state. Many white residents of Los Angeles and other cities up and down the Pacific Coast expressed heightened fears that African Americans, people of Mexican descent, and other minorities did not share their appreciation for American customs or their sense of patriotism. Of all these minorities, Mexican-American workers, families, and communities were regarded by white Angelenos with particular distrust. Their uneasiness was fed not only by racist stereotypes that had been passed down from generation to generation, but also by more recent developments.

In the late 1930s and early 1940s the sheer number of Mexican Americans and Mexican immigrants in Los Angeles and its surrounding region had grown significantly. Like workers of every other ethnicity, they came to take advantage of a wartime economy that had shifted into high gear in 1939, when World War II began in Europe and America agreed to provide England and other Allied nations with military arms and other supplies. These wartime job opportunities had become even more lucrative after the attack on Pearl Harbor, when the United States entered the war.

All told, an estimated two million Mexican-American workers relocated during the war to California, where many of the country's major shipyards and aircraft manufacturers were located. Whites still received preferential treatment over workers of Mexican descent in these bustling defense factories, which made the rifles, jeeps, planes, submarines, and other materials needed by U.S. armed forces. But many Mexican Americans did manage to secure employment in the defense industry, albeit in lower-paying jobs. From 1941 to 1944, for example, the number of Mexican Americans working in Los Angeles shipyards jumped from almost zero to more than 17,000. In addition, the fast-growing defense industry attracted so many Anglo workers that non-defense industries and businesses had to admit greater numbers of Mexicans and African Americans to their payrolls to keep their doors open.

The Rise of the Zoot Suit

Another factor responsible for escalating white anxieties about Mexicans was a social phenomenon that was taking place all across the city during the early 1940s. Like several other large American cities of the era, Los Angeles experienced a wave of youthful rebellion that greatly disturbed older generations. One of the trademarks of this rebellion was a love for swinging jazz music, which conservative, older Anglo Americans viewed as a sign of slipping morality. As scholar Eduardo Obregón Pagán wrote, "Jazz was to white Americans in the 1940s what rock and roll was in the 1950s and rap was in the 1980s."[2]

Critics thought that jazz and swing—a high-energy, big band variation of jazz—encouraged sexual promiscuity and drinking among young people. Even worse in the eyes of many, the theaters and nightclubs where this music was featured showed a complete disregard for longstanding rules of racial segregation. "Race mixing on and off the stage and dance floor was common, and in the age of segregation, such a violation of white supremacy was an outrage," said Pagán. "As a behavior spreading among the youth, it was perceived as a social danger."[3]

The most visible symbol of this cultural revolt by young people, though, was their enthusiasm for a radical, exaggerated version of the traditional business suit known as the zoot suit. The zoot suit featured long coats with wide padded shoulders and lapels, as well as high-waisted, pleated pants that bil-

American jazz bandleader Cab Calloway sports a zoot suit while performing in 1935.

lowed around the knees before narrowing down to a tight fit around the ankles. The so-called zoot suiters also favored thick-soled shoes, broad-brimmed hats, suspenders and narrow belts, long watch chains that swung from vest or pants pockets, and long hair that was combed back in an "Argentinian" style to form a thick wedge or "duck tail" at the back of the head.

A female version of the zoot suit also took shape in the late 1930s and early 1940s. It featured the same wide-shouldered, tapered coats that male zoot suiters favored, but it substituted pleated skirts and black hose for pants. Women zoot suiters also gravitated to attention-grabbing hairstyles. Many of them piled their hair in exaggerated waves or pompadours on top, then let the rest of their hair fall loosely around their shoulders. Female zoot suit fashions never got quite as outrageous as the male versions, though, and they never received as much attention from critics.

The exact origins of the zoot suit have been difficult to pinpoint. Frank Walton, who directed the federal government's efforts to conserve clothing material during World War II, spoke for many when he said that "many attempts have been made to analyze the idea [of the zoot suit] and to see just what caused it and what was behind it but so far there is no good answer."[4] Historians believe, though, that the zoot suit, which was also sometimes called "the drape," originated in the mid-1930s in African-American communities in New York and other Eastern cities. Jazz artists based on the East Coast then spread it across the country as they toured. Each region of the country put its own distinctive stamp on the fashion. Eastern zoot suiters, for example, preferred much more colorful suits than their western counterparts. All across the country, though, zoot suit culture symbolized excitement, pleasure, and youthful defiance of the expectations of parents and wider society. "Like youth of any generation, the zoot suit was a symbol of one's own generational style," explained George Sanchez, who came to adulthood in Los Angeles during the zoot suit era. "This was to really assert that, you know, we are here, and we want to make a statement about the fact that we're here. But it was also, I think, a connection with other minority and poor youth in the United States."[5]

As Sanchez indicated, zoot suiters could be found in American working-class neighborhoods of all ethnicities. The outfit was popular with young African Americans on both coasts, as well as Filipino Americans and Japanese Americans along the Pacific Coast. Zoot suits were also sported by Italian Americans and Irish Americans from mixed-race working-class neighborhoods. In the West, though—and especially in Los Angeles—the most visible champions of so-called "zoot suit culture" were young Mexican Americans.

Young zoot suiters of Hispanic heritage in Los Angeles offered a variety of reasons for their attraction to the zoot suit lifestyle. Many saw it as a fun and even glamorous escape from the drab reality of their daily existence. For some young men, wrote Pagán, "putting on the zoot [suit] was nothing less than a rebirth of identity, transforming him from an awkward country boy who couldn't dance to the bezooted hipster who exploded on to the dance floor in the rhythmic fury of the lindy hop.... His zoot was a public signal that he had gone from square to cool, from awkward to hip. He was born a new man."[6]

Others saw the zoot suit culture as something that was uniquely their own, a creation that could not be taken away by overbearing parents or racist white authorities. It was a declaration of self-worth by a socioeconomic group that was at the mercy of older Anglo lawmakers, business owners, and police in most other aspects of life. The rise of the zoot suit was a sign that Mexican-American and African-American youth no longer accepted being relegated to the shadows of American society.

A teenager shows off his zoot suit in the early 1940s.

Pachucos in the Barrio

Many of the Hispanic youth within Los Angeles's zoot suit culture were law-abiding young men and women. They attended school, worked full-time or after-school jobs, and hung out with their friends at local pool halls, malt shops, or house parties in much the same manner as their non-zoot suit-wearing neighbors. The young people who did own zoot suits, meanwhile, usually saved them for special occasions, such as birthday celebrations or excursions to the fancy downtown swing clubs.

The reputation of the zoot suits was altered, though, by the rise of a *Pachuco* subculture that enthusiastically adopted the zoot suit as a standard uniform of sorts. Among Mexican Americans, the word *Pachuco* was a hostile slang term for rough, uneducated Mexican workers from El Paso, Texas, and Ciudad Juárez, Mexico, who migrated to California in the 1920s and 1930s. These emigrants from the Texas border country spoke their own dialect of Mexican Spanish, and they were not always fully accepted by Mexican-American Californios. Over time, California-born Mexican Americans started using the term when referring to any Hispanic who was rude, vulgar, or a troublemaker.

By the late 1930s, however, some Mexican-American youths were voluntarily identifying themselves as Pachucos (or *Pachucas,* in the case of females). These teens and young men and women felt disconnected from their Mexican heritage but also resisted assimilation into wider American society. They were left unsupervised for long afternoons by fathers and older brothers who had gone off to fight in the war and mothers who worked long hours to support their families. Yet they had few ways to pass their idle hours in a city that restricted most of its recreational opportunities to white residents. Bored and disillusioned, these youths increasingly engaged in petty crime and organized themselves into loose street gangs. These groups, in fact, are regarded by historians as the early forerunners of the dangerous Latino gangs that currently menace some American communities.

Over time, the Pachucos developed a perverse pride in behaving in ways that shocked or outraged the society that kept them at arm's length. Taking note of the controversy surrounding zoot suits, many Pachucos made sure that they had one (or more) hanging in their closets. They also self-consciously rejected the standards of "proper" behavior held by their parents and community in favor of a swaggering, "hipster" attitude. "The hipster carried the air of the trickster about him, of a man living by his wits, enjoying life on his own terms, existing for the constant edge of excitement and pleasure," wrote Pagán. "Hookers and marijuana were rumored to be his constant companions and defiant manhood his creed."[7]

Mexican writer, diplomat, and Nobel Prize winner Octavio Paz lived in Berkeley, California, during the war. In his view, the behavior of the Pachucos reflected a desperate need for the rest of the world to take notice of them. "[The Pachuco] knows that it is dangerous to stand out and that his behavior irritates society, but nevertheless he seeks and attracts persecution and scandal," he wrote. "As a victim, he can occupy a place in the world that previously ignored him; as a delinquent, he can become one of its wicked heroes."[8]

A Hostile White Response

By the early 1940s the lines between Mexican-American zoot suiters and Pachucos had become blurred, with considerable overlap between the two groups. As Pagán observed, however, "not every Pachuco wore a 'zoot suit,' and not every Mexican American who combed his hair in the Argentinean style … or who wore 'drapes' was a Pachuco."[9]

During this period, though, few white Californians cared about such distinctions. They increasingly used the term Pachuco to refer not only to hoodlums and gang members within the Hispanic community, but to any Mexican American wearing a zoot suit. In other words, any Mexican-American teenager who strayed outside the lines of "appropriate" behavior, as defined by white

U.S. sailors on leave and their dates enjoying a night on the town in downtown Los Angeles in 1943.

Angelenos, came to be viewed as a juvenile delinquent and—sooner or later—a likely threat to law-abiding citizens.

Not all white residents adopted this view. Anglos who opposed the city's segregationist structure and those who actually interacted with Hispanics in their neighborhoods or workplaces were less likely to accept this stereotype. But the city's white-dominated press and police department were less willing to entertain the idea that Hispanic youth were not all cut from the same zoot-suited cloth. In fact, the press and the police increasingly regarded all Mexican-American youth—and especially male teens—not as potential contributors to society, but as potential recruits for Pachuco gangs.

Finally, many whites regarded the wearing of a zoot suit—whether it was draped across the body of a Mexican American or any other young man—as an unpatriotic act. These angry feelings were based on the fact that during World War II, the U.S. government rationed many products on the home front. Under this system, each American was only entitled to a limited amount of goods and materials that were in short supply during wartime, including gasoline, meat, sugar, coffee, and tires. This conservation program was designed to help make sure that the nation's soldiers, sailors, and marines received the supplies they needed, and to spread the sacrifice of popular foods and other material comforts across the entire American population.

Wool fabric for civilian clothing was also strictly rationed during the war so that manufacturers would have enough material to meet the military's needs for uniforms, blankets, and other woolen items. When these rationing regulations were handed down in early 1942, established clothing manufacturers stopped making zoot suits because they required more fabric than ordinary business suits. Demand for zoot suits remained high, though, and some tailors in Los Angeles and New York kept making the suits. They then sold the suits on the "black market," a secretive and illegal market in goods.

The continued sight of zoot suiters on the streets of Los Angeles thus became a source of great frustration to some white Angelenos. As historian Stuart Cosgrove wrote, "The zoot-suit was a moral and social scandal … not simply because it was associated with petty crime and violence, but because it openly snubbed the laws of rationing."[10] This view of zoot suiters was also widely held by the white sailors, soldiers, and marines who were stationed in the many military bases that existed outside the city. When servicemen on leave from these bases visited the clubs and bars of downtown Los Angeles, the sight of "unpatriotic" zoot suiters sometimes triggered verbal or physical attacks.

Tensions in the Barrio

The reaction to Los Angeles's zoot suit culture within the Mexican-American community was more complex. Most Hispanic residents of the city—95 to 97 percent by one estimate—never wore a zoot suit in their lives.[11] Many families, though, had a member or an acquaintance who owned a zoot suit, so they did not view the fashion in quite the same negative light as did white Angelenos. If the zoot suiter was someone who had grown up on your block, attended your church, or sat at your dinner table, you were less likely to view him as an alien menace.

Nonetheless, zoot suiters and Pachucos were regarded warily by many members of the Mexican-American community. Many older residents of the barrio viewed the zoot suit as a foolish fad that cast an embarrassing light on their people. They also expressed growing concern that the fashion was contributing to outbreaks of violence between rival neighborhood gangs. Some Hispanics—and especially those whose fathers, sons, or brothers were in the wartime military—also shared Anglo feelings that zoot suits were inherently unpatriotic.

"Many older barrio residents viewed the zoot suit as a foolish fad that cast an embarrassing light on their people. Some Hispanics—and especially those whose fathers, sons, or brothers were in the wartime military—also shared Anglo feelings that zoot suits were inherently unpatriotic."

Meanwhile, rivalries developed in many Hispanic neighborhoods between the zoot-suit crowd and what the Pachucos sneeringly called the "Pepsi-Cola kids"—Mexican-American teens who studied hard, had friendships with Anglo kids, and stayed out of trouble. In the worst cases, these tensions erupted into ugly incidents of violence and taunting. Scholar Anthony Macias also noted, however, "that many squares lived side-by-side with the Pachucos on friendly terms."[12]

The most prominent critics of zoot-suit culture within Los Angeles's Mexican-American community were members of the city's small but politically active Hispanic middle-class. By the early 1940s, these doctors, lawyers, and business owners had created a number of organizations dedicated to improving the lives and the public image of Mexican Americans in Los Angeles and throughout the West and Southwest. Sometimes these organizations carried out campaigns to educate Anglo Californians about the economic and artistic contributions made by Hispanics. On other occasions, community leaders fought against negative stereotyping of Mexican Americans in the press. In addition, Mexican-American community organizations sponsored services and recreational opportunities for Hispanic youth, including boys' and girls' clubs, counseling services, and athletic teams.

Another major focus of groups like the League of Latin American Citizens (LULAC) and the Coordinating Council for Latin American Youth (CCLAY) was to make the case for "cultural pluralism"—the idea that Mexican Americans could be loyal Americans and still treasure their cultural history and traditions. Mexican-American activists like Manuel Ruíz Jr., an attorney who founded CCLAY, worked tirelessly for what Macias described as "the full acceptance and integration of Mexican Americans into all levels of U.S. society as first-class citizens, without the loss of their cultural heritage and ethnic identity."[13]

Manuel Ruíz Jr. and the Coordinating Council for Latin American Youth

One of the leading voices representing the Mexican-American community in World War II-era Los Angeles was the Coordinating Council for Latin American Youth (CCLAY), which was led by Manuel Ruíz Jr. The son of Mexican immigrants, Ruíz was born on July 25, 1905, in Los Angeles. He received a law degree from the University of Southern California and earned his state law license in 1930, but racial discrimination kept any of the established white law firms in town from offering him a job. Undaunted, Ruíz established his own law practice in Los Angeles.

Ruíz also became a noted social activist for Hispanics in the late 1930s and early 1940s. His knowledge of the law and dynamic personality made him a leading figure in groups like the Coordinating Council for Latin American Youth (CCLAY), a coalition of youth groups that worked to improve educational and employment opportunities for Hispanic boys and girls. The organization also represented the city's Mexican-American community in numerous clashes with the white-controlled city government and business district. "Ruíz and the Coordinating Council were active in youth job programs, desegregation issues, defense against racial prejudice, and political action," wrote scholar Richard Griswold del Castillo. "The Council acted as a watchdog, filing complaints when they found evidence of violation of federal guidelines regarding employment and housing, and complaining to the Los Angeles newspapers that continued to publish derogatory and stereotypical portrayals of Mexican-American youth as pachucos."

This quest for equality, however, was made more difficult by the controversy that swirled around the zoot suiters. To older generations of Mexican Americans, the zoot suiters seemed like an irresponsible and self-absorbed lot who simply did not care whether their antics cast the wider Hispanic community in a negative light. Parents, meanwhile, fretted that zoot suit culture threatened to lure their children down a dark path. "As young Mexican Americans stepped out in their zoot suits," remarked one documentary on the Zoot Suit Riots, "their parents saw their children disappearing into a different world, and they feared their kids would become ill-mannered 'pachucos.'"[14]

Ruíz became even more prominent after the Zoot Suit Riots of 1943. He emerged as a kind of go-between for the city's white leadership and its Mexican-American community. Tired of the indiscriminate use of the term "Mexican" for any person of Hispanic background, he was one of the first people to urge adoption of the terms "Latino" or "Americans of Latin background" to remind whites that Mexican Americans were full-fledged citizens of the United States. At times Ruíz helped white authorities identify Mexican-American youth that he believed were guilty of instigating violence during the riots. As historian Eduardo Obregón Pagán wrote, though, he also "appealed for greater understanding between racial groups and [supported] a progressive agenda he believed would bring about a postwar society of greater tolerance."

The CCLAY faded away after the war, its advocacy role taken over by other organizations. Ruíz, however, remained a prominent law figure in Los Angeles for the next several decades. He also remained heavily involved in issues related to Hispanic youth, and from 1970 to 1980 he served as a member of the U.S. Commission for Civil Rights. Ruíz died in 1986.

Sources:

del Castillo, Richard Griswold. "Civil Rights on the Home Front." In *World War II and Mexican-American Civil Rights.* Edited by Richard Griswold del Castillo. Austin: University of Texas Press, 2008, pp. 84-88.

Pagán, Eduardo Obregón. *Murder at the Sleepy Lagoon: Zoot Suits, Race, and Riot in Wartime L.A.* Chapel Hill: University of North Carolina Press, 2003, pp. 196-98.

Incident at Sleepy Lagoon

As concerns about zoot suiters, Pachucos, and wayward Mexican-American youth escalated across wartime Los Angeles, a murder took place that seemed to confirm the worst fears of the city's white population. The crime was committed on the night of August 1, 1942, on a ranch located on the southeastern outskirts of Los Angeles. Within a matter of days, seventeen Mexican-American teens and young men had been arrested and charged with involvement in the crime. As details of the case leaked out in the city's dominant white newspapers over the next several weeks, many readers—including leading officials in the L.A. Police Department—concluded that the murder personified everything that was wrong was the city's Hispanic community.

For the seventeen young men charged, the night of August 1 had actually begun quietly. Several young Hispanic couples from the city's 38th Street barrio had decided to go that evening to Sleepy Lagoon, a big reservoir outside of Los Angeles that was a favorite romantic destination. The lagoon was part of the Williams Ranch, a big agricultural outfit in the area that relied heavily on Mexican-American field hands.

One of the couples from the 38th Street neighborhood at the lagoon was a young man named Henry "Hank" Leyvas (see Leyvas biography, p. 137) and his girlfriend, Dora Barrios. They were sitting quietly in Leyvas's car when a drunken group of young white men cruised by, shouting insults at the couple. These young men from the neighboring town of Downey had just been ejected from a house party that was being held at a bunkhouse elsewhere on the Williams Ranch. The party had been organized by Amelio and Angela Delgadillo, a Mexican-American couple who worked on the ranch, to celebrate the twentieth birthday of their daughter, Eleanor Delgadillo Coronado. The Delgadillos and several of their Mexican-American friends had kicked out the "Downey boys"—who had shown up uninvited in the first place—after they became rowdy and obnoxious.

When Leyvas heard the insults from the Downey youths, he stepped out of his car and hurled some insults back. The Downey car continued on down the dirt road, though, so it appeared that the incident was not going to amount to much. About a half-hour later, though, a larger group of Downey youths returned to the lagoon under cover of darkness. They attacked Leyvas with their fists and boots, and when Barrios tried to shield her boyfriend from the onslaught, the attackers began beating her as well. A few other youths from 38th Street rushed to the aid of their friends when the sounds of the attack reached their ears. They were severely outnumbered, though, and before long they were forced to retreat and hide in the cornfields to avoid a vicious beating themselves.

After about fifteen minutes the Downey boys finally ended their attack and left the scene, their taunting voices echoing in the minds of their victims. The battered residents of 38th Street promptly returned to their neighborhood and gathered reinforcements for a revenge attack on the youths who had attacked them. By the time they piled in their cars to return to Sleepy Lagoon, Leyvas had almost forty young men and women with him. As Pagán wrote, they believed "that the assault on Henry and Dora by a group required a group response. Clearly they could not let an assault on their peers go unpunished, but they were more likely outraged by the nature of the attack. Badly outnumbered, none of the boys stood a chance of defending themselves." Even worse, the fact that Dora had been repeatedly punched and kicked "was an egregious violation of their fundamental sense of morality."[15]

A New Spasm of Violence at the Williams Ranch

When Leyvas and the 38th Street group returned to Sleepy Lagoon, there was no sign of the Downey attackers. Someone in the party then suggested that some of the attackers might be at the Delgadillo party. The 38th Street group promptly drove to the Delgadillo home, where the party was dying out. Leyvas and a handful of his friends parked their cars and strode up to a gate leading to the Delgadillo bunkhouse. They were met there by Eleanor Delgadillo Coronado, who was still enjoying the last minutes of her birthday party, and her brother-in-law, Cruz Reyes.

Leyvas immediately demanded to know where his attackers were hiding, which led a puzzled Coronado to respond that most of the partygoers were gone. At that point Leyvas brushed past her and threw a punch at Reyes. The reason for this attack has long been a point of debate among investigators and historians, who point out that Reyes had nothing to do with the initial assault on Leyvas and Barrios. It may have been a case of mistaken identity, or Reyes might have acted in a way that Leyvas interpreted as threatening or aggressive. The possibility also exists that Leyvas was just so angry and frustrated at that point in the night that he was willing to fight just about anyone if it would allow him to release his emotions.

A 1942 portrait of Henry "Hank" Leyvas, a central figure in the Sleepy Lagoon murder mystery.

Whatever the reason, Levyas's assault on Reyes triggered a full-scale brawl between the 38th Street young people and the Delgadillo family and friends. As the ugly fight escalated, teen girls and women slashed at each other with bottles and fists, and some members of the 38th Street crowd ganged up on their outnumbered foes with just as much viciousness as the Downey men had displayed earlier in the evening. One of the worst offenders was José "Chepe" Ruíz, who beat one partygoer into unconsciousness, then pounded on his victim's body with a two-by-four wooden board until he was stopped by a couple other 38th Street residents. Another offender was Ysmael "Smiles" Parra, who struck Eleanor Coronado during the melee, then attacked her father when he tried to defend his daughter. As the brawl continued, other youths from 38th Street shot the tires and smashed the windows of the parked cars that belonged to the Delgadillos and their remaining guests.

The attack ended when someone yelled that the police were on their way. The crowd of teens and twenty-somethings from 38th Street promptly jumped into their cars and sped away, leaving behind an assortment of dazed and bloodied victims. Amelio Delgadillo instructed his family and friends to search the grounds surrounding the bunkhouse to make sure that no one needing medical attention was missed. A short time later, searchers came upon the unconscious form of one of their guests, José Díaz (see Díaz biography, p. 128). His face and body were bruised and bloody and his pockets were turned inside out as if he had been robbed. According to some reports, he also had stab wounds in his abdomen.

During the forty-five-minute ambulance ride to Los Angeles General Hospital, Díaz hovered in a semiconscious state, unable to answer more than a few basic questions. When he was admitted, doctors at the hospital diagnosed him with a severe cerebral concussion in addition to his other injuries. They tried to save him, but Díaz died an hour and a half after his arrival.

Under ordinary circumstances, Díaz's death might not have attracted much attention. Over the next several months, though, it became clear that the city of Los Angeles—and its Hispanic population in particular—would be forever changed by his death.

Notes:

[1] Quoted in Peiss, Kathy. *Zoot Suit: The Enigmatic Career of an Extreme Style.* Philadelphia: University of Pennsylvania Press, 2011, p. 115.

[2] Pagán, Eduardo Obregón. *Murder at the Sleepy Lagoon: Zoot Suits, Race, and Riot in Wartime L.A.* Chapel Hill: University of North Carolina Press, 2003, p. 98.

[3] Pagán, p, 99.

[4] Peiss, p. 2.
[5] Quoted in "Zoot Suit Culture." In *The American Experience: Zoot Suit Riots,* 2002. Retrieved from www.pbs.org/wgbh/amex/zoot/eng_sfeature/sf_zoot.html.
[6] Pagán, pp. 116-17.
[7] Pagán, pp. 120-21.
[8] Paz, Octavio: *The Labyrinth of Solitude: Life and Thought in Mexico.* New York: Grove Press, 1985, p. 16.
[9] Pagán, p. 36.
[10] Cosgrove, Stuart. "The Zoot-Suit and Style Warfare." *History Workshop Journal,* Autumn 1984, pp. 77-91. Retrieved from invention.smithsonian.org/centerpieces/whole_cloth/u7sf/u7materials/cosgrove .html.
[11] Pagán, p. 39.
[12] Macias, Anthony. *Mexican-American Mojo: Popular Music, Dance, and Urban Culture in Los Angeles, 1935-1968.* Durham, NC: Duke University Press, 2008, p. 102.
[13] Macias, p. 97.
[14] Quoted in "People and Events: Clem Peoples and the Los Angeles Police Department." In *The American Experience: Zoot Suit Riots,* 2002. Retrieved from www.pbs.org/wgbh/amex/zoot/eng_ peo pleevents/p_lapd.html.
[15] Pagán, p. 63.

Chapter Four

THE TRIAL OF THE 38TH STREET BOYS

From the beginning the proceedings [in the Sleepy Lagoon murder case] savored more a ceremonial lynching than a trial in a court of justice.

—Carey McWilliams, *North from Mexico*

Under normal circumstances the murder of José Díaz would not have attracted that much attention. New murder cases were investigated by police every day in huge metropolitan areas like Los Angeles, and few of them elicited headlines for more than a day or two. The police and press gave extra attention to murder cases that involved rich or famous individuals, but Díaz did not fit either of these descriptions. Only twenty-two years old at the time of his death, the Mexican immigrant had spent the previous several years working in the California fields. He then decided to enlist in the armed services, like millions of other young Americans did during World War II. Díaz was killed, in fact, the weekend before he was scheduled to report for induction into the U.S. Army. His death was a tragic event for his family and friends, but his anonymous working-class background was similar to that of many other murder victims in Los Angeles that year.

The timing of Díaz's death, though, changed everything. His body was discovered at a time when leading officials in Los Angeles and the state capital of Sacramento were expressing growing concern about youth crime among minority populations in California's larger cities. When authorities learned that Díaz's body had been found in the vicinity of a bloody melee between two Mexican-American factions, they used his death as evidence that a statewide crackdown on youth gangs and juvenile delinquency was needed.

Crackdown on Youth Gangs

When California's Democratic governor, Culbert L. Olson, took office in January 1939, white anxiety about the impact of immigrants and minorities on American society had emerged as one of his biggest challenges. He wholeheartedly supported the internment of Japanese Americans after Pearl Harbor. Olson asserted that since it was impossible to tell loyal Japanese Americans from traitors, "the wholesale evacuation of the Japanese people from coastal California"[1] was a sensible precaution. Olson also repeatedly expressed concerns about rising levels of juvenile delinquency in California.

By the time José Díaz was murdered, the Olson administration was actively looking for opportunities to prove its dedication to stamping out crime and dismantling youth gangs. Top officials in the Los Angeles Police Department (LAPD) and the Los Angeles County Sheriff's Department (LACSD) felt the same way. Authorities thus used Díaz's death to justify a major crackdown on juvenile crime in Los Angeles. In the days following the opening of the murder investigation, police swept through Mexican-American and African-American neighborhoods.

The police crackdown unfolded in methodical fashion, according to journalist and civil rights activist Carey McWilliams (see McWilliams biography, p. 141). "If one spreads out the span of one's right hand and puts the palm down on the center of a map of Los Angeles County with the thumb pointing north, at the tip of each finger will be found a community where the population is predominantly Mexican," he wrote in *North from Mexico*.

> In each of these neighborhoods, moreover, a majority of the juveniles living in the area will be found to be first-generation Mexican-Americans, sons and daughters of the Mexican immigrants who came to Southern California during the 1920s. The police selected the neighborhoods which lay at our fingertips on the maps and then blockaded the main streets running through these neighborhoods. All cars containing Mexican occupants, entering or leaving the neighborhoods, were stopped. The occupants were then ordered to the sidewalks where they were searched. With the occupants removed, other officers searched the cars for weapons or other illicit goods.[2]

By the time the dragnet had concluded, an estimated 600 young men and women had been detained by police. Many of the young people taken into custody were described as zoot suiters and Pachucos.

This dragnet received approving coverage in the *Los Angeles Times*, the *Los Angeles Herald-Express*, and other popular newspapers and magazines. Their stories about the so-called "Sleepy Lagoon Murder" and the subsequent police investigation reflected not only the "public fascination with juvenile delinquency," noted historian Eduardo Obregón Pagán, but also the "growing perception that working-class youths were caught up in a zoot-suited crime wave sweeping the city."[3]

Investigating the Sleepy Lagoon Murder

Over the next several weeks investigators were able to piece together many of the events that had taken place at Sleepy Lagoon and the Williams Ranch on the night that Díaz was killed. Armed with eyewitnesses from the Delgadillo party, they also were able to identify many of the young men and women from 38th Street who had been involved in the Williams Ranch brawl. Before long, police investigators were focusing most of their energy on Leyvas and thirty or so other male residents of the 38th Street neighborhood. Strangely, however, they never followed up on a statement from Eleanor Delgadillo Coronado that she had seen Díaz leave the party with two other male partygoers about ten to twenty minutes before the 38th Street crowd arrived at the ranch. She identified both of the young men, but investigators apparently never brought them in for questioning or ever regarded them as suspects.[4]

The 38th Street residents who became the target of the police investigation had a mixed criminal history. Many of the young men already had minor criminal offenses on their records, and several of them had been convicted of robbery, car theft, assault with a deadly weapon, and other more serious crimes by the time they reached their eighteenth birthdays. As a result, Levyas and several other 38th Street "hoodlums" were well known to the police before the Díaz investigation even began. On the other hand, some of the young men under investigation had never been in trouble before. Others had been rounded up by the police during one investigation or another, only to be released after police determined that they were innocent.

As the weeks passed by, police became frustrated by the refusal of 38th Street residents to give information that might implicate their friends in the actual murder. This uncooperative stance reflected strong neighborhood loyalties, but it also stemmed from the extremely poor relations that existed between Los Angeles police and the city's minority populations. Mexican

Eight of the estimated 600 young Mexican-American Angelenos who were taken into police custody following the Sleepy Lagoon murder.

Americans frequently complained of brutal and humiliating treatment from white officers—and even of mistreatment from Hispanic police who wanted to "prove themselves" to their white colleagues. On two previous occasions, for example, Los Angeles police had picked up one of the Díaz murder suspects—Benny Alvarez—on suspicion of automobile theft. "The first time he was held for five hours and the second time for eighteen weeks—all this despite the fact that he owned the car in question," reported Pagán. "During one of these arrests, the officers slapped and pistol-whipped him with the butt of a gun."[5]

The barrios of Los Angeles also contained a multitude of stories about white officers sexually harassing Hispanic girls and women, white officers kicking Mexican Americans out of predominantly white neighborhoods, and Hispanic youths receiving jail sentences based on false or trumped-up charges. Finally, historians believe that the young people from 38th Street who were taken into custody may not have revealed the identity of Díaz's murderers for the simple reason that they did not know who committed the crime.

As the investigation dragged on, the detectives in charge of the Díaz case were accused on several occasions of resorting to beatings and intimidation to elicit confessions from the 38th Street suspects. Anna Zacsek, who served as the attorney for Leyvas and three other 38th Street suspects, charged that on one occasion she visited the jail and found that investigators had left Leyvas "slumped forward in a semiconscious state, with his shirt dappled from the blood and saliva that fell from his swollen lips and bleeding nose."[6] The police department flatly denied all accusations that officers had struck or otherwise mistreated anyone connected with the Sleepy Lagoon case.

Convening a Grand Jury

As the Díaz murder investigation continued, a Los Angeles County grand jury was convened to review the case and decide whether formal charges should be brought against the 38th Street suspects. As the grand jury considered the evidence, though, it also was exposed to fierce debates about the causes and severity of Mexican-American juvenile delinquency in Los Angeles and other American cities.

The first wave of people who spoke out on the issue were high-ranking officers from the LAPD and LACSD, all of whom expressed a belief that juvenile crime among Mexican Americans was on the rise in Los Angeles. Several of these chiefs admitted that life in the barrio was significantly harder for young people than life in affluent white homes and communities. They insisted, however, that poverty, discrimination, overcrowding, and educational segregation were only minor factors in the rise of the Pachuco. The officers argued that the basic nature of Mexican Americans made them more likely to engage in criminal behavior.

All of the law enforcement officials who testified before the grand jury offered some version of this racial theory to explain California's "Mexican problem." But the man who made the case most strongly was Lieutenant Edward Duran Ayres, chief of the Foreign Relations Department of the Los Angeles Coun-

An August 10, 1942, court appearance of the twenty-three Mexican-American youths indicted by Los Angeles County authorities in the Sleepy Lagoon slaying.

ty Sheriff's Department. In both a formal report and grand jury testimony, Ayres strove to link modern-day Hispanics to the ancient Aztec civilization that practiced human sacrifice (see "A Los Angeles Police Officer Issues a Racist Report on the Mexican 'Element,'" p. 164). In his view, Mexican-American youths had an Aztec-like disregard for human life. Ayres also insisted that Mexicans and other non-Anglo races were genetically and morally inferior to Anglos.

Ayres's testimony and written report reflected prejudices that were dominant among young officers and veteran police commanders (and numerous white citizens) at the time. His calls for relentless crackdowns on Mexican-American neighborhoods and long prison sentences for juvenile offenders also reflected the viewpoint of the wider Los Angeles police community. The solution to youth crime in the barrio, agreed other law enforcement officials who appeared before the grand jury, was to reject leniency and pursue a policy of "swift and sure punishment" until the "Latinos" realized that Los Angeles would not tolerate "gangsterism."[7] According to these voices, the Díaz case presented a golden opportunity to show the city's youth gangs that the authorities meant business.

"Delinquency is not a monopoly of any racial or national group," testified labor analyst Guy T. Nunn. "It is a monopoly of poverty, excessive housing concentration, social and economic discrimination. These, far more than juvenile delinquency, characterize our Spanish-speaking minority."

The authority of Ayres and his allies was accepted by most members of the grand jury. Two jurors, however, felt that the testimony had been unfairly slanted against the Sleepy Lagoon defendants as well as the city's Mexican-American population. One of these jurors was Charlotta Bass, editor of the black-owned newspaper *California Eagle* and the first African-American woman ever to serve on a Los Angeles County grand jury. The other was Harry Braverman, a labor activist with strong Socialist views. Braverman in particular was so incensed by the police testimony that he successfully pushed for a second grand jury hearing to hear statements in opposition to the so-called Ayres Report.

This second hearing was held on October 8, 1942. It included testimony from McWilliams, a prominent critic of California's historical treatment of the state's Indian and Hispanic populations. The grand jury also heard from Mexican-American and African-American activists who argued that the problem of youth crime in Los Angeles could best be solved by tearing down the discriminatory walls that kept these groups from fully entering American society. They also emphasized that young Mexican Americans felt that street gangs gave them a sense of pride and belonging that could not be found in a white-dominated society that looked down on their cultural and racial heritage.

This perspective was echoed by Guy T. Nunn, a labor analyst with the National Labor Relations Board and the War Manpower Commission. "Delinquency is not a monopoly of any racial or national group," Dunn stated. "It is a monopoly of poverty, excessive housing concentration, social and economic discrimination. These, far more than juvenile delinquency, characterize our Spanish-speaking minority."[8]

Going to Trial

Although the grand jury that was convened for the Sleepy Lagoon case became deeply engaged in arguments about how and why—or even whether—youth crime was on the rise in minority neighborhoods of Los Angeles, their ultimate responsibility was to decide whether the 38th Street defendants should be charged with a crime. Unlike regular juries, which require unanimous consent to determine guilt or innocence, members of grand juries do not require a unanimous decision in deciding whether to file criminal charges. Some grand juries, in fact, only require a simple majority. In the end, the Sleepy Lagoon grand jurors decided to recommend an indictment on first degree "conspiracy to commit murder" charges against twenty-two young men (the final vote was not made public).

The grand jury decided against recommending charges against the girls and young women who had been involved in the fight at the Williams Ranch. It was widely acknowledged that some of them had been in the thick of the brawl, but the jurors evidently decided that the 38th Street boys and young men posed a greater threat to the city. In addition, the prosecutors may have hoped that by sparing the girls, they might be able to convince them to provide testimony against the boys.

The prosecution was led by assistant district attorneys (DAs) Clyde Shoemaker and John Barnes, who had the full resources of the city's District Attorney's Office at their disposal. The defense team that came together to represent the twenty-two defendants, on the other hand, consisted of an assortment of individual lawyers who were each only responsible for defending a few of the 38th Street boys. A "public defender"—a lawyer paid by the government to represent defendants who could not afford to hire a lawyer themselves—was assigned to represent six of the young men. His name was Richard F. Bird. Several other lawyers were hired by the families of the defendants to represent their sons as well. The most prominent of these attorneys was Anna Zacsek. Her handful of clients included Leyvas, who by this time had been identified by prosecutors as the ringleader of what they called the "38th Street Gang."

The judge who drew the assignment for the Sleepy Lagoon case was Los Angeles County Superior Court judge Charles William Fricke (see Fricke biography, p. 131). The defense lawyers did not view Fricke's selection as a positive development for their cause. Fricke was known around the courthouse as "San Quentin Fricke" because he had sentenced more people to the state's notorious San Quentin maximum-security prison than any other judge in California.

Accused of Being a Gang

The trial was officially known as *California v. Zammora et al.* (defendant Gustavo Zamora—whose name was misspelled in the legal documents—was chosen by lottery to be the first person listed). By the time it opened on October 13, 1942, five of the defendants—Edward Grandpré, Ruben Peña, Daniel Verdugo, Joe Carpio, and Richard Gastelum—had successfully appealed for separate, individual trials (all five were eventually acquitted of all charges). The number of defendants in the mass *California v. Zammora* trial thus dwindled from twenty-two to seventeen.

George Shibley led a spirited defense of the Sleepy Lagoon defendants, challenging the judge's pro-prosecution bias throughout the trial.

Within a few days it became clear to court watchers that the defense team had been unable to come up with a legal strategy to which all members could agree. Instead, each attorney focused on defending his or her respective clients rather than the group as a whole. As a result, the defense lawyers regularly quarreled with each other. The defense effort was also hurt by the fact that several of the attorneys had only limited courtroom experience.

The defense performed so badly, in fact, that one of the city's most vocal defenders of the 38th Street boys stepped in. Midway through the trial, labor organizer LaRue McCormick convinced distinguished defense attorney George Shibley (see Shibley biography, p. 148) to replace Bird. Technically, Shibley was only responsible for representing Bird's six defendants. His arrival, though, brought a much-needed burst of energy and skill that lifted the entire defense team.

The prosecution, meanwhile, had problems of its own. Since it had no eyewitnesses to the Díaz murder and no murder weapon, it was forced to base its entire case on the fact that the defendants had instigated a huge brawl in the same area in which the dying Díaz had been found. The prosecution recognized that the all-white jury of six women and four men would give heavier weight to this knowledge if they viewed the seventeen defendants as members of a genuine "gang." With this in mind, they spent a lot of time labeling the defendants as a "38th Street Gang" commanded by Leyvas.

Sleepy Lagoon trial judge Charles Fricke issued numerous rulings that benefited the prosecution and hampered the defense.

The defense strongly objected to this description. Shibley and his colleagues noted that the 38th Street residents on trial did not have any formal leadership system, illegal money making operations, or public displays of membership. Without any of these usual gang hallmarks, they asked, how could the defendants be legitimately defined as gang members? The defense also countered this line of attack through the testimony of other residents of the 38th Street neighborhood. When asked if the term "38th Street Gang" meant anything to her, one of the young women who had been at the Williams Ranch on the night of Díaz's murder responded that "it means just a group of kids that are known to each other and run around with each other. … I mean, if kids from a different neighborhood ask me where I am from, I will say '38th,' because that is the group I run around with."[9]

This testimony reflected the overall stance of all the young women from the 38th Street neighborhood. They refused to cooperate with the prosecution at any point in the trial. The frustrated prosecutors responded to their defiance by sending several of them, including Hank Leyvas's girlfriend, Dora Barrios, to a state reformatory for girls. On average the girls remained in the reformatory, which operated much like a military camp, for sixteen months. Even after their release, they remained under state supervision until they turned twenty-one. Some supporters of the 38th Street boys visited the girls during their incarceration, but no campaign to gain their release ever took shape. "The [Hispanic] community's silence over the fate of the Sleepy Lagoon girls," wrote Pagán, "may have resulted from the belief that these women … got precisely what they deserved."[10]

Controversial Rulings Hamper the Defense

The defense team's other main problem was Fricke, who issued a series of rulings that greatly benefited the prosecution. Citing courtroom space considerations, the judge forced the defendants to sit far away from their lawyers when court was in session. He only allowed the lawyers to confer with their clients during breaks or after court had adjourned for the day. Fricke also refused to allow the defendants to cut their hair or change out of the clothing they wore in jail for the first several weeks of the trial. Fricke's ruling, wrote McWilliams, forced "the defendants [to come] trouping into the courtroom every day looking like so many unkempt vagabonds."[11] Many historians have agreed with this assessment. Scholar Mauricio Mazón, for example, wrote that the defendants were displayed to the jury as if they were exhibits in a "carnival freak show."[12]

Fricke also displayed unmistakable hostility toward Shibley, who made effective use of objections and other courtroom maneuvers against the prosecution. As the trial wore on, observed one documentary overview of the trial, "Fricke increasingly demeaned Shibley and the defendants in front of the jury, thereby reducing their credibility and any hope for a fair trial."[13] Undaunted, Shibley continued to file legal objections to various court proceedings. He knew that if the defendants were found guilty, these objections could serve as the basis for an appeal of the verdicts (see "Courtroom Clashes between Fricke and Shibley," p. 168).

The efforts of Shibley and the other members of the defense team, though, were also hampered at times by the courtroom behavior of the defendants. As the long trial continued, some of the defendants displayed expressions of cockiness or boredom that did not help their cause. At times they poked at each other and threw spit wads as if they were bored kids in a classroom, not young men on trial for murder. These antics further worsened the perceptions of the all-white jury, according to Alice Greenfield, who assisted Shibley during the trial. "The hostility of the jury was almost palpable," she recalled. "You could see that they were looking at the defendants as though they were loathsome."[14]

The Trial Becomes a Media Sensation

As the Sleepy Lagoon trial progressed, the Los Angeles press became much more heavily engaged in covering the proceedings. When the trial first opened, the city's major newspapers provided only brief updates, reasoning that the public was not all that interested in the fate of a bunch of Mexican-American boys from the barrio. Over time, however, the editors and publishers of these publications came to realize that the trial's minority gang-related themes might actually resonate with its mostly white readership.

Newspaper magnate William Randolph Hearst owned the *Los Angeles Herald-Express*, which was hostile to the defense throughout the Sleepy Lagoon trial.

By mid-trial, most of the city's newspapers and tabloid magazines were splashing their front pages with breathless accounts of the proceedings. Unfortunately for the defense, much of this coverage was sensationalistic and heavily slanted against the defendants. Most of the papers, for example, barely mentioned the defense's persistent claim that Díaz might not have been murdered at all; his injuries, they asserted, were consistent with those of someone who had been hit by a car. The press also routinely referred to the 38th Street defendants as a gang, even though that description had been hotly contested by Shibley and the other lawyers for the defense.

The papers and magazines, which were made available to the jury throughout the trial, also used the terms Pachuco and zoot suiter interchangeably with words like gangster, mobster, hoodlum, and killer. "The police and the press, often working in tandem, bore a particular responsibility for shifting the meaning of the zoot suit from a harmless, if extreme, phenomenon to a symbol of deviance and danger," wrote scholar Kathy Peiss. Despite the fact that whites, blacks, and Asian Americans also wore zoot suits in early-1940s America, "among the newspaper-reading public [of Los Angeles], the Sleepy Lagoon coverage and everyday crime beat made *zoot suit* and *zoot suiter* almost exclusively the symbols of young Mexican-American delinquents and offenders."[15]

Historians say that the *Los Angeles Herald-Express*, which was owned and managed by conservative newspaper magnate William Randolph Hearst, showed the most blatant favoritism toward the prosecution. From the beginning, it described the defendants with phrases like "the goons of Sleepy Lagoon."[16] The single most infamous example of the prejudicial coverage of the trial, though, was probably a December 1942 issue of *Sensation* magazine. This issue featured a long article titled "Smashing California's Baby Gangsters" by Clem Peoples, chief of the Criminal Division of the Los Angeles County Sheriff's Department. Peoples described the 38th Street defendants as "reckless mad-brained young wolves" who posed a dire threat to the good, law-abiding people of Los Angeles.

The cumulative impact of this news coverage on the public was significant. By the time the trial came to a close in early 1943, some white residents of Los Angeles had become more convinced than ever that the city was on the verge of being swamped by a zoot-suited Hispanic crime wave. In addition, the high-profile trial intensified white doubts about whether "Mexican citizens and their American-born children were culturally, politically, intellectually, and biologically capable of living within a white, civilized democratic society."[17] Meanwhile, the press made no mention of developments that did not fit its narrative—such as the fact that the crime rate among minority youths in Los Angeles during the last months of 1942 had actually gone down.[18]

Sentencing of the 38th Street "Gang"

On January 12, 1943, the Sleepy Lagoon trial came to a close and the jury retreated to consider the evidence. When the jurors returned, they came armed with guilty verdicts for all seventeen defendants. As the verdicts were read, many of the defendants and their family members in the courtroom burst into tears.

With these verdicts in hand, Fricke imposed prison sentences that surprised even some veteran prosecutors. Fricke sentenced the three men found guilty of first-degree murder—Henry Leyvas, José "Chepe" Ruíz, and Bobby Telles—to life imprisonment. Nine other defendants found guilty of second-degree murder were sentenced to five years to life in prison. These men were Ysmael "Smiles" Parra, Manuel Reyes, Victor "Bobby" Thompson, Henry Ynostroza, Gus Zamora, Manuel Delgado, John Matuz, Jack Melendez, and Angel Padilla. The last five defendants (Andrew Acosta, Eugene Carpio, Victor Segobia, Benny Alvarez, and Joe Valenzuela) were convicted of assault, but they were released because of the amount of time they had already served in jail. All twelve of the young men who were convicted of murder were immediately transported to San Quentin to begin serving their sentences.

Supporters of the seventeen Sleepy Lagoon defendants expressed frustration with the outcome of the trial and Fricke's stiff sentences, but they vowed to continue the legal fight on behalf of Leyvas and the other inmates. During the course of the trial McCormick had established a group called the Citizens' Committee for the Defense of Mexican-American Youth (CCDMAY) to rally

Police investigator Clem Peoples (at left) published a highly publicized attack on Los Angeles's young Mexican-American community in the midst of the Sleepy Lagoon trial.

public support for the defendants and bring attention to Fricke's handling of the case. Now, with the trial over and the 38th Street boys in prison, McCormick and several of her allies reorganized the committee into the Sleepy Lagoon Defense Committee (SLDC).

The goal of the SLDC was clear: to raise money to fund an appeal of the convictions by publicizing what they termed the "poisonous atmosphere"[19] at the trial. The group was helmed by Chairman Carey McWilliams and Executive Secretary Alice Greenfield (see Greenfield biography, p.), but it also included representatives of assorted labor and church groups, Communist activists, prominent African-American and Hispanic community leaders, and attorneys and scholars with a strong interest in constitutional rights issues. The SLDC even received support from famous film stars such as Orson Welles, Rita Hayworth, and Anthony Quinn.

The SLDC knew that it was fighting an uphill battle. In the eyes of its members, the 38th Street boys had been railroaded into prison via a trial that had treated them as guilty from the outset. In many respects, though, Leyvas and the other "Pachucos" who had been convicted of Díaz's murder were unsympathetic figures. Their criminal records and boorish behavior during the trial assured much of the public of their guilt, and Los Angeles residents of every race were reluctant to question law enforcement agencies in the middle of a war that called for national unity.[20]

Finding support for their cause was difficult even within California's Mexican-American community. As historian Frank P. Barajas stated, "Many parents of the emerging Mexican-American generation viewed the pachucos as troublemaking *mechudos vagos* (long-haired bums) who sullied the community's reputation."[21]

As it turned out, however, the SLDC devised an ingenious fundraising argument that was also sincerely believed by many of its members. The organization charged that instead of being the *source* of dissension and turmoil in America, the 38th Street defendants and many other Hispanic and African-American men and women were *victims* of fascist newspaper publishers and authorities who were themselves sowing distrust and division in wartime America.

Notes:

1 Quoted in "Olson Wants All Japs Moved." *San Francisco News,* March 6, 1942.
2 McWilliams, Carey. *North from Mexico: The Spanish-Speaking People of the United States.* New York: Lippincott, 1949.
3 Pagán, Eduardo Obregón. *Murder at the Sleepy Lagoon: Zoot Suits, Race, and Riot in Wartime L.A.* Chapel Hill: University of North Carolina Press, 2003, p. 72.
4 "People and Events: José Gallardo Díaz (1919-1942)." In *The American Experience: Zoot Suit Riots,* 2002. Retrieved from http://www.pbs.org/wgbh/amex/zoot/eng_peopleevents/p_diaz.html.
5 Pagán, pp. 57-58.
6 Pagán, p. 74.
7 Quoted in Leonard, Kevin Allen. *The Battle for Los Angeles: Racial Ideology and World War II.* Albuquerque: University of New Mexico Press, 2006, p. 163.
8 Quoted in Leonard, p. 97.
9 Pagán, p. 82.
10 Pagán, p. 203.
11 McWilliams, p. 230.
12 Mazón, Mauricio. *The Zoot Suit Riots: The Psychology of Symbolic Annihilation.* Austin: University of Texas Press, 1984, p. 20.
13 "People & Events: Judge Charles Williams Fricke (1882-1958)." In *The American Experience: Zoot Suit Riots,* 2002. Retrieved from http://www.pbs.org/wgbh/amex/zoot/eng_peopleevents/p_fricke.html.
14 Quoted in "The Education of Alice McGrath." Michael Balter, interviewer. Los Angeles: Oral History Program, University of California, Los Angeles, 1987.
15 Peiss, Kathy. *Zoot Suit: The Enigmatic Career of an Extreme Style.* Philadelphia: University of Pennsylvania Press, 2011, p. 114.
16 Dibbern, Doug. "The Violent Poetry of the Times." In *"Un-American" Hollywood: Politics and Film in the Blacklist Era.* Edited by Frank Krutnik, et al. Newark, NJ: Rutgers University Press, 2008, p. 98.
17 Pagán, p. 3.
18 Pagán, p. 92.
19 Quoted in "Honorable in All Things Oral History Transcript: The Memoirs of Carey McWilliams." Joel Gardner, interviewer. Los Angeles: Oral History Program, University of California, Los Angeles, 1978.
20 Barajas, Frank P. "The Defense Committees of Sleepy Lagoon: A Convergent Struggle against Fascism, 1942-1944." *Aztlán: A Journal of Chicano Studies,* Spring 2006, p. 44.
21 Barajas, pp. 43-44.

Chapter Five

THE ZOOT SUIT RIOTS

> It sure is terrible, what's going on in L.A. I never dream that … that thing's [sic] like that would happen in the U.S.A., a land of Freedom.[1]
>
> —Sleepy Lagoon defendant Manuel Reyes, in a June 16, 1943, letter to Alice Greenfield from San Quentin Prison

At the same time as the Sleepy Lagoon Defense Committee (SLDC) was getting organized, press-fueled anxiety about youth crime triggered another wave of police actions in Mexican-American and African-American neighborhoods across Los Angeles. Police roundups of young people—and especially zoot suiters and Pachucos—escalated in early 1943, to the applause of white Angelenos who had avidly followed the Sleepy Lagoon murder trial. Officers expanded their raids on house parties in these neighborhoods, broke up outdoor gatherings of minorities in public parks and other settings, and increased their arrests of young minorities for loitering. According to the people who were taken into custody in these and other police actions, physical abuse of inmates in the city and county jails remained a common occurrence.

Rising Tensions with White Servicemen

During this same period, longstanding tensions between Hispanic Angelenos and white members of the U.S. armed forces continued to worsen. During World War II the West Coast was home to a large number of U.S. military bases that served two purposes: to train new sailors, soldiers, and marines for the war, and to defend the United States against possible attack from Japan. The majority of these bases were located in southern California, around and between the cities

Although most servicemen on weekend leave, such as this soldier dancing at Los Angeles's Hollywood Canteen, enjoyed downtown L.A. without incident in the early 1940s, others got in ugly clashes with minority youth.

of Los Angeles and San Diego. Both cities thus became favorite destinations of servicemen who were "on leave"—on approved absences from their bases.

As a result, the streets of Los Angeles filled every weekend with up to 50,000 servicemen who were eager to "partake of the excitement of Hollywood and the California lifestyle and to simply get away from the drudgery of military confinement."[2] On their way to and from the nightclubs and bars of downtown Los Angeles, though, the sailors, soldiers, and marines passed through Mexican-American neighborhoods that bordered the bases. In addition, Hispanic youths and white servicemen and their girlfriends frequented many of the same nightlife venues in the city's entertainment district.

Many of these young men and women shared Los Angeles's public spaces without any problems. They just wanted to enjoy themselves and spend time with their friends in a city that was renowned for its nightlife. Nonetheless, clashes between Hispanics and white servicemen became progressively more common and serious.

These encounters were fed in part by excessive alcohol consumption. Another key factor was white unfamiliarity with Hispanics. Servicemen from many parts of the country had never been around Spanish-speaking people before. Unlike African-American soldiers who were segregated into separate military units, Mexican Americans did serve in white units. However, they only accounted for about two to five percent of the U.S. Armed Forces during the war.

Probably the biggest factor in the growing violence between the two camps, though, was that both white servicemen and Mexican-American boys and men attached a great deal of importance to appearing "manly," "tough," and capable of defending the honor of "their" women.

Ugly Incidents on the Rise

During and after the Sleepy Lagoon trial, hostilities between Hispanics and military men seemed to grow with each passing week. Mexican Americans sometimes sexually harassed white girls and women, but white servicemen directed the same ugly taunts and groping at Mexican-American girls. Sailors, marines, and soldiers making their way back to base after a night of partying were sometimes waylaid by Mexican-American or African-American youth who beat them up and robbed them. White servicemen, meanwhile, frequently roughed up minorities whether they were wearing zoot suits or not.

Los Angeles was not the only California city in which these explosions of race-based violence occurred. In April 1942, for example, white marines and sailors invaded several Mexican-American and African-American neighborhoods in Oakland, where they assaulted a number of zoot-suited residents. Eight months later, a race riot involving more than 200 black and white sailors erupted in Vallejo, a city in the San Francisco Bay area. In San Diego, meanwhile, city councilman Charles C. Dail, who later became mayor of that city, reported that white servicemen in the area were being threatening and obnoxious to *all* civilians, black, brown, or white. "There have been numerous instances in San Diego where members of the military forces have insulted and vilified civilians on public streets,"[3] he wrote in a letter to the commanders of a nearby naval base.

The main arena for these clashes, though, remained Los Angeles. One zoot suiter who grew up in the city recalled that fights between Mexican Americans and white servicemen were just an ordinary part of life for himself and his friends during the war years. "At that time I was fourteen, fifteen years old," he said. "Oh man, I got in a lot of fights with soldiers and sailors and marines."[4]

A Sign of Things to Come

In May 1943 the flames of racial tension in Los Angeles flared up to new heights. One evening in Venice, a beachfront district on the west side of Los Angeles, a false rumor began circulating among white sailors, high school students, and other civilians that a white sailor had been stabbed by zoot suiters. Outraged white men gathered together on the streets and beat up a group of Mexican-American zoot suiters when they exited a nearby ballroom to head home. Unsatisfied, the fast-growing mob started cruising the streets, attacking any young Hispanic men they encountered. "They didn't care whether the Mexican kids wore zoot suits or not," said one eyewitness. "They just wanted Mexicans."[5]

Zoot suiters in Venice organized a series of counterattacks, and before long white and Hispanic youths and men were beating on each other all over the area. The riot spiraled out of control, spilling over into neighboring Santa Monica. The battle ended only after police moved in and began taking zoot suiters into custody.

The fact that the police targeted Hispanics rather than whites—who had started the melee, after all—outraged the zoot suiters. One policeman later claimed that the officers felt that arresting the Mexican-American participants in the brawl was the only way to defuse the crisis. "Servicemen have no regard for civilian police officer control. Our actions are limited by what the public thinks. The sailors and high-school kids got hold of rumors. Everybody was upset with jittery emotions wanting to let off steam. So you had a riot, and the zoot suiters were the safety valve. You'll admit the only thing we could do to break it up was arrest the Mexican kids."[6]

"Servicemen have no regard for civilian police officer control," said one Los Angeles police officer. "Everybody was upset with jittery emotions wanting to let off steam. So you had a riot, and the zoot suiters were the safety valve. You'll admit the only thing we could do to break it up was arrest the Mexican kids."

The Fateful Spark That Launched the Riots

Historians trace the beginning of the actual Zoot Suit Riots to the evening of May 31, when a group of a dozen or so sailors and soldiers clashed with a larger cluster of zoot suiters in the downtown district. The fight, which apparently started because the Hispanic youths took offense at the servicemen's interest in a group of young Mexican-American women, turned into a rout. Outnumbered, the battered and bloody servicemen were forced to make a chaotic retreat, dragging along the body of one unconscious sailor named Joe Dacy Coleman.

News of the assault—and especially of Coleman's injuries—spread to bases all around Los Angeles. According to this version of events, the servicemen were assaulted without provocation by a vicious gang. According to the zoot suiters, meanwhile, Coleman and his pals had started the fight, only to get more than they bargained for. Whatever the truth of the matter, the brawl had lasting repercussions.

On June 3 a group of about fifty revenge-minded sailors from Coleman's command at Chavez Ravine Armory left the base and marched to the nearby Alpine neighborhood, where clashes between servicemen and Mexican-American youth had often occurred in the past. One Navy officer later admitted that the intentions of the servicemen were clear: "We knew where they were going and the guards [who could have stopped them at the gates] looked the other way. Most thought it was high time something was done."[7] Unable to find zoot suiters on the street, the frustrated sailors entered a local movie theater and attacked Hispanic patrons. "Roaming up and down the aisles, the sailors pulled boys from their seats, while others administered unmerciful beatings," wrote historian Solomon James Jones. "In several cases men were taken from the side of their wives, children, and parents."[8]

A short time later, a group of Mexican-American boys—some dressed in zoot suits, some not—returned to Alpine from a nearby police station, where they had attended a meeting on reducing juvenile delinquency and gang violence in their community. When the sailors saw the zoot suiters, they immediately set upon them. They beat them up, tore their suits off, and set their clothing on fire in the middle of the street. Not even the younger boys (some were no more than twelve years old) were spared from this ordeal. "Exhausting the supply of Pachuco victims from the street, sailors [then] poured into beer parlors and restaurants, hunting at random,"[9] wrote Jones.

The rioting mob continued to swell in size as the hours passed, its ranks replenished by other servicemen who caught wind of what was happening and joined in. The violence of June 3 did not ebb until late in the night, after members of the city police and navy shore patrol (whose primary responsibility is to keep sailors on leave out of trouble) finally arrived on the scene and detained a number of rioting sailors. Later that night, however, all the sailors were released to go back to their base without any charges filed against them.

Days of Fear and Violence

The release of the sailors without any punishment contributed to a movement among Los Angeles-area servicemen to repeat the zoot-suit bashing of June 3 on the following night. The prospect of launching another offensive against the city's zoot suiters—who had been consistently portrayed in the press as subversive menaces to American stability and morality—was extremely appealing to strong young men who had been trained to go to war in defense of their nation. According to Alice Greenfield, "It was [as] though the frustration of not being able to go over and kill Japs, or whatever it was that they [the

American sailors and marines armed with bats roam the streets of Los Angeles looking for zoot suiters in the early days of the Zoot Suit Riots.

navy] were building them up to [do],"[10] led the sailors to identify the zoot suiters as an alternative target.

On the night of Friday, June 4, about 200 sailors left the Armory in a convoy of taxi cabs. They directed the drivers to the heart of the Mexican-American neighborhoods of East Los Angeles and Boyle Heights, where they knew they would find zoot-suited young men. In other words, observed one documentary account, the servicemen launched "an assault on the Mexican-American community itself. The sailors cruised the barrio, storming into bars, cafes, and theaters."[11] Los Angeles police and Navy shore patrol personnel made little effort to rein in the servicemen as they carried out their angry manhunt for zoot suiters.

As the weekend of June 5 and 6 approached, the riots captured the attention of the city's press. All of the major newspapers trumpeted the clashes from earlier in the week on their front pages. In virtually all of these stories, the writers framed the actions of the servicemen as an understandable and even admirable response to months of outrages committed by "zoot-suit gangsters."

The military bases that dotted the outskirts of Los Angeles thus became a hotbed of excitement as the evening of Saturday, June 5, approached. "Los Angeles seethed with preparation," wrote Jones. "As word passed along the grapevine, weekend passes were hurriedly issued to sailors, marines, and soldiers who rushed to Los Angeles to join in battle."[12] Scholars have generally agreed that the military's decision to issue these passes despite the violence of the previous few nights showed a stunning disregard for the safety of the city's Mexican-American citizenry—and perhaps even tacit approval of the actions of the servicemen.[13] Representatives of the city's Hispanic community, meanwhile, asked for additional protection from the police, the shore patrol, and the military police (each branch of the armed services maintains its own police force), but to no avail.

On the night of June 5, servicemen descended on Los Angeles once again in a quest to beat up Mexican-American zoot suiters and rip their clothes to shreds. On several occasions they punched and stripped Mexican-American zoot suiters to the sounds of cheers from white onlookers (see "Trying to Survive the Zoot Suit Riots," p. 173). Mexican-American youth scattered at the sight of the servicemen, but they did not always get away, as this account from a reporter for the *Los Angeles Examiner* attests:

> Thirty-six blue jackets [sailors] in six automobiles conducted a landing at First and State streets. A gang of zooters sighted them and fled into a nearby dance hall, and mingled with the two hundred patrons. The sailors followed and obtained their objective. Zooters were crawling about with battered heads and smashed noses.... Next the navyboys set sail for a bar at Brooklyn Avenue and Indiana Street where fifty pachucos were hiding. The bar was in bad shape and so were the zooters when the navy left.[14]

This violence and intimidation outraged many people in Los Angeles. Some whites joined African Americans and Mexican Americans in complaining that attacking zoot suiters was a betrayal of American ideals. "This is supposed to be a free country," said one Mexican-American sailor. "We don't go around beating up people just because we don't like the clothes they wear."[15]

The beatings resulted in a downturn in the number of Hispanic youths who dared to go downtown, especially dressed in their "drapes." Some frustrated rioters responded to the shortage of downtown prey by marching into the barrios again. Law enforcement showed virtually no interest in stopping the invasion of the Mexican-American neighborhoods. Military police (MPs) and shore patrol officers were overwhelmed by the size of the mobs, and the city and county police forces remained remarkably passive. As *Time* magazine noted in a report on the escalating Los Angeles riots, "the police practice was to accompany the caravans [of rioting servicemen] in police cars, watch the beatings, and jail the victims."[16] On a few occasions where it appeared that Mexican-American youth might be organizing to launch a counterattack, patrolling policemen warned them to disperse or face arrest.[17] "In other instances," charged the Los Angeles Committee for American Unity in a post-riot investigation, "police actually participated in the brutal beatings that occurred."[18]

The white mob left non-zoot-suited citizens alone for the most part, but Hispanic witnesses to their bullying and violent behavior were still terrified. And on a few occasions, military men attacked Mexican Americans who were not wearing zoot suits at all. The best known of these incidents was a completely unprovoked attack on a group of adult Hispanic musicians as they departed the Aztec Recording Company studios in downtown Los Angeles.

A City in Chaos

The following night, June 6, brought a fourth consecutive invasion of the city's Hispanic enclaves. For the first time the gangs of white servicemen were joined by significant numbers of white civilians. As the evening wore on, the rioters expanded their circle of targets to include African Americans. Beatings of Hispanic and black youth flared up all across the city, and once again the city's police refused to intervene. "Many of us were in the first world war, and we're not going to pick on kids in the service," said one officer. "Most citizens thought it was a good idea anyway"[19] to go to war against the zoot suiters.

On this night, though, the first significant stirrings of Mexican-American defiance could also be seen. Some Hispanic youth organized violent counterattacks against civilians and servicemen. One zoot suiter recalled that he and

Servicemen cruise the streets of Los Angeles and show off "trophies" of clothing torn from zoot suiters.

his friends became accomplished at using decoys to lure white military men and civilians into alleyways and buildings where zooters waited in ambush. "And they [the white servicemen and civilians] let out a cry: There they are! There they are! And they came in. As they came in, once they got all the way in, we all came out.... I, myself, had a bat. And I used it."[20]

Monday, June 7, brought the worst fighting of all. Hundreds of servicemen from as far away as San Diego and Las Vegas traveled to Los Angeles to join in the riots. Historians estimate that the mob grew to include as many as 5,000 servicemen and civilians that night. As the evening wore on, the white mob not only seized control of the downtown district, it also sent contingents deep into nearby Hispanic and African-American neighborhoods. Residents of these neighborhoods watched in fear as their communities were invaded by thick clots of armed servicemen and civilians. Racially charged mob violence also broke out in other parts of California, including San Diego, Pasadena, and Long Beach.

A Mexican-American zoot suiter shows off a black eye and torn clothing, the results of an attack by American servicemen in Los Angeles on June 8, 1943.

U.S. military officials and city leaders finally acted to end the chaos on Tuesday, June 8. Up to this point commanders of the nearby bases had hoped that the rioting would die out on its own. They were stunned by the breakdown in military discipline that had taken place, but they also feared the public embarrassment that would accompany any mass arrests of disorderly sailors, soldiers, or marines. As scholar Mauricio Mazón pointed out, "if they [had] exercised decisive and immediate authority, according to the provisions under the Uniform Code of Military Justice, they would have had to incarcerate and court-martial hundreds and perhaps thousands of servicemen for disorderly conduct, disobeying direct orders, inciting a riot, being AWOL [absent without leave], and, conceivably, mutiny."[21]

In the early hours of June 8, though, area base commanders received yet another wave of reports describing Los Angeles as a city awash in racial violence and "disorderly" servicemen. One senior shore patrol officer reported that "hundreds of servicemen [are] prowling downtown Los Angeles on foot—disorderly—apparently on prowl for Mexicans.... Los Angeles Police have called in all off-duty men and auxiliary police to handle situation.... Groups vary in size from 10 to 150 men and scatter immediately when shore patrol approach."[22]

These reports finally roused the commanders to action. They issued explicit orders to base personnel to stay out of Los Angeles. The first and most important of these orders was issued by Admiral David W. Bagley, commandant of the 11th Naval District. Bagley described the ban as a "precautionary measure" and he insisted that the sailors had only been acting in "self-defense against the rowdy element" over the previous several nights. Nonetheless, Bagley's order specifically declared Los Angeles to be "out of bounds" to all enlisted sailors.[23]

Other Race Riots of 1943

The Zoot Suit Riots that rocked Los Angeles were just the first of a series of race riots that erupted across the United States in the summer of 1943. As the summer progressed, race riots broke out in Chicago, Illinois; Detroit, Michigan; Harlem, New York; Philadelphia, Pennsylvania; Mobile, Alabama; Baltimore, Maryland; Washington, D.C.; and Beaumont, Texas. In most of these cases, falsehoods or exaggerated tales of racial violence spread among black or white populations, triggering actual outbreaks of race-based assaults and murders. Military servicemen were major participants in several of these outbreaks, just as they had been in Los Angeles.

None of these later riots lasted as long as the one in Los Angeles, but several of them were much deadlier. The rioting in Detroit, for example, lasted for three days (June 20-June 22) and resulted in the deaths of 34 people.

These orders brought a quick end to the rioting. The full-scale battles and vicious beatings that had marked the previous five days declined to a few minor skirmishes. With servicemen holed up in their bases, the civilians who had participated in the weekend rioting went back to their normal lives as well. In the meantime, local law enforcement joined with military police and shore patrol personnel to patrol the now-quiet streets. "By the morning of June 8," wrote Jones, "Los Angeles had acquired the semblance of a city under martial law."[24]

A Dazed City Takes Stock

Once the Zoot Suit Riots subsided, everyone who had been affected by the violence rushed forward to advance their interpretation of the week's events. The city's big newspapers had actively encouraged the drive to "punish" Los Angeles's "zoot-suit gangsters," and they had glorified the entire affair. "Huge half-page photographs, showing Mexican boys stripped of their clothes, cowering on the pavement, often bleeding profusely, surrounded by jeering mobs of men and women, appeared in all the Los Angeles newspapers,"[25] noted one post-riot investigation.

Afterward, however, the press—and its supporters in the business community—belatedly sensed that the racial aspects of the rioting were damaging

The ongoing Zoot Suit Riots finally convinced Rear Admiral David W. Bagley to issue a June 8, 1943, order for all U.S. Navy personnel to stay out of Los Angeles.

the city's reputation. In an effort to repair the damage, several papers hastily printed editorials assuring the world that racial tensions in Los Angeles were exaggerated. As the *Los Angeles Daily News* wrote on June 11, "every true Californian has an affection for his fellow citizen of Mexican culture that influence our way of living, our architecture, our music, our language, and even our food."[26] And when First Lady Eleanor Roosevelt publicly referred to the troubles in Los Angeles as a race riot, the *Los Angeles Times* responded by issuing an angry condemnation of Roosevelt (see "The *Los Angeles Times* Attacks Eleanor Roosevelt's Stance on the Riots," p. 177).

The response of city officials was muddled. On the one hand, the city council approved a June 9 resolution that banned the wearing of zoot suits on Los Angeles streets. Anyone who violated the new measure could be thrown in jail for fifty days. However, Mayor Fletcher Bowron (see Bowron biography, p. 125) insisted that neither the Zoot Suit Riots nor the anti-zooter resolution should be interpreted as a sign of ugly racial resentments or hostilities. "Nothing has occurred," he said, "which could be construed as due to prejudice against Mexicans or discrimination against youths of any race."[27]

Back at the military bases, servicemen tried to convince both themselves and the wider world that their actions in Los Angeles had been a necessary response to the city's Pachuco gangs. "Our intent of taking justice in our own hands was not an attempt to instill mob rule but only the desire to ensure our wives and families safe passage in the streets," wrote one group of sailors in a letter to the *Los Angeles Daily News*. "Our past activities we realize were not within the law but we are sure that they met with the honest approval of the people."[28]

Military commanders, meanwhile, focused on making sure that their commands would never again fall victim to such a dramatic breakdown in military discipline. On June 11 Major General Maxwell Murray, commander of the Southern California Sector Western Defense Command, issued a memorandum

A Warning to West Coast Servicemen

By June 9, 1943, the Zoot Suit Riots in Los Angeles were over, but criticism of the role U.S. sailors, soldiers, and marines played in the unrest was just starting to roll in. As the condemnation increased, military leaders in California vowed that no similar events would flare up again under their watch. On June 11, for example, Major General Maxwell Murray issued a stern warning to the army personnel under his command all across southern California. Murray's memorandum emphasized the following points:

1. The recent incidents connected with the so-called "Zoot-Suit" riots involved mob action, and incipient rioting, by many soldiers and other servicemen.

2. Prompt action to check such action has been taken, charges are being preferred against those arrested for inciting or actually participating in these riots.

3. It is obvious that many soldiers are not aware of the serious nature of riot charges. Convictions in a recent serious riot have resulted in sentence to death or long confinement.

4. It is desired that the attention of all Military personnel be called immediately to the critical dangers of any form of rioting and that incidents which may start as thoughtless group action in comparatively trivial offenses or boisterous conduct are liable to develop into mob riots of the serious character. Further, mob rioting usually results in injury to persons in no way connected with initial cause of the disorder. This is true in the case of the recent disorders which resulted in affront and injury of some completely innocent civilians.

5. Military personnel of all ranks must understand that no form of mob violence or rioting will be tolerated, and that offenses of this nature will result in immediate and drastic disciplinary action.

Source:

Memorandum 6-11-43 [memorandum from Major General Maxwell Murray to Headquarters, Southern California Sector, Western Defense Command]. *Zoot Suit Discovery Guide.* Retrieved from research.pomona.edu/zootsuit/en/resources/newspaper-articles/memorandum-6-11-43/.

"It is significant that most of the persons mistreated during the recent incidents in Los Angeles were either persons of Mexican descent or Negroes," the McGucken Report stated. "In undertaking to deal with the cause of these outbreaks, the existence of race prejudice cannot be ignored."

tersely warning all military personnel that mob violence and rioting would not be tolerated.

Military officials, though, also blamed Los Angeles's city police and sheriff's officers for the lawlessness that had descended on the city over the previous week. They charged them with negligence in their handling of the riots and pointed out that the military base commanders had no authority over the civilians who had taken part in the rioting. The police and sheriff's department defended themselves against these criticisms by pointing out that servicemen had been at the center of the rioting throughout. They also said that if the military had kept all men on base during the weekend of June 5-6, the riots never would have reached such serious heights.

Reactions to the riots in the city's Mexican-American community were mixed. Some older barrio residents disliked the Pachucos and openly lamented the violence that sometimes erupted between youth gangs. The invasion of their neighborhoods by marauding white servicemen and civilians, though, had greatly shaken them. Younger Mexican Americans, meanwhile, described the riots as an ordeal that obviously had been rooted in racial hatred. This viewpoint was echoed by civil rights groups like the Coordinating Council for Latin-American Youth and the Los Angeles Committee for American Unity. Both of these organizations blamed the riots on a corrosive combination of irresponsible press coverage, longstanding racial animosities, incompetent police work, and poor military leadership (see "Mexican-American Activists Assess the Causes of the Zoot Suit Riots," p. 174).

The McGucken Report

Stung by these criticisms of his state—and by condemnations from national publications, members of Congress, and even the government of Mexico—California governor Earl Warren ordered the creation of a citizens' commission to investigate the cause of the riots. He appointed Catholic bishop Joseph T. McGucken to lead the investigation. On June 13, the so-called McGucken Report was released. To the dismay of Bowron and many business leaders in Los Angeles, McGucken and his colleagues declared that racism against Mexican Americans and African Americans had been an obvious and major factor in the riots: "It is significant that most of the persons mistreated during the recent incidents in Los Angeles were either persons of Mexican descent or Negroes. In undertaking to deal with the cause of these outbreaks, the existence of race prejudice cannot be ignored."[29]

The McGucken Report embarrassed the city in other ways as well. It detailed the poor living conditions and job discrimination that Mexican Americans endured every day in Los Angeles, and it pointed out that these conditions created fertile soil for juvenile delinquency. The commission also criticized the press and police for their relentlessly negative attitudes toward the city's Mexican-American community. "Mass arrests, dragnet raids, and other wholesale classifications of groups of people are based on false premises," it stated. "Group accusations foster race prejudice, the entire group accused want revenge and vindication. The public is led to believe that every person in the accused group is guilty of crime."[30]

Finally, the commission scolded whites in Los Angeles and across California for their overreaction to the zoot-suit fashion trend. "The wearers of zoot suits are not necessarily persons of Mexican descent, criminals or juveniles," stated the report. "Many young people today wear zoot suits. It is a mistake in fact and an aggravating practice to link the phrase 'zoot suit' with the report of a crime."[31]

Notes:

1 Reyes, Manuel "Manny." Letter to Alice Greenfield, June 16, 1943. *Calisphere* [Web site]. Los Angeles: Sleepy Lagoon Defense Committee records, University of California, Los Angeles. Retrieved from content.cdlib.org/view?docId=hb8z09p55v&query=&brand=calisphere.

2 Mazón, Mauricio. *The Zoot Suit Riots: The Psychology of Symbolic Annihilation.* Austin: University of Texas Press, 1984, p. 66-67.

3 Quoted in Mazón, p. 71.

4 Alvarez, Luis. *The Power of the Zoot: Youth Culture and Resistance during World War II.* Berkeley: University of California Press, 2008, pp. 157-58.

5 Escobar, Edward. *Race, Police, and the Making of a Political Identity: Mexican Americans and the Los Angeles Police Department, 1900-1945.* Berkeley: University of California Press, 1999, p. 230.

6 Quoted in Griffith, Beatrice. *American Me*. Boston: Houghton Mifflin, 1948, p. 19.

7 Quoted in Griffith, p. 20.

8 Jones, Solomon James. *The Government Riots of Los Angeles, June 1943: A Thesis.* Los Angeles: University of California, Los Angeles, 1969, p. 24.

9 Jones, p. 25.

10 Quoted in "The Education of Alice McGrath." Michael Balter, interviewer. Los Angeles: Oral History Program, University of California, Los Angeles, 1987.

11 Quoted in "The Zoot Suit Riots: People and Events." In *The American Experience: Zoot Suit Riots,* 2002. Retrieved from www.pbs.org/wgbh/amex/zoot/eng_peopleevents/e_riots.html.

[12] Jones, p. 26.
[13] Jones, p. 26.
[14] Quoted in Jones, pp. 27-28.
[15] Quoted in Peiss, Kathy. *Zoot Suit: The Enigmatic Career of an Extreme Style*. Philadelphia: University of Pennsylvania Press, 2011, p. 115
[16] *Time*, June 21, 1943, p. 29.
[17] Jones, p. 27.
[18] Los Angeles Committee for American Unity. "Investigations of the Zoot-Suit Riots," June 1943, p. 3. In Jones, Solomon James. *The Government Riots of Los Angeles, June 1943: A Thesis*. Los Angeles: University of California, Los Angeles, 1969, pp. 42-43.
[19] Quoted in Griffith, p. 23.
[20] Quoted in "The Zoot Suit Riots: People and Events." Retrieved from www.pbs.org/wgbh/amex/zoot/eng_peopleevents/e_riots.html.
[21] Mazón, p. 73.
[22] "Official Military Memoranda Concerning Zoot Suit Riots." In *The Home Front Encyclopedia: United States, Britain, and Canada in World Wars I and II*. Edited by James Ciment. Thousand Oaks, CA: SAGE, 2007, p. 1284.
[23] "City, Navy Clamp Lid on Zoot Suit Warfare." *Los Angeles Times*, June 9, 1943. Retrieved from research.pomona.edu/zootsuit/en/resources/newspaper-articles/city-navy-clamp-lid-on-zoot-suit-warfare/.
[24] Jones, p. 32.
[25] *Governor's Citizen's Committee Report on Los Angeles Riots*, 1943. As quoted in Mintz, Steven, ed. *Mexican American Voices: A Documentary Reader*. Malden, MA: Wiley-Blackwell, 2009, p. 161.
[26] Quoted in Jones, p. 37.
[27] Quoted in Escobar, p. 246.
[28] Quoted in Jones, p. 33.
[29] *Governor's Citizen's Committee Report on Los Angeles Riots*. Quoted in Mintz, Steven, ed. *Mexican American Voices*, p. 161.
[30] Ibid.
[31] Quoted in "Los Angeles Group Insists Riots Halt." *New York Times*, June 13, 1943.

Chapter Six

RELEASE FROM PRISON

> Hysterical screams and shrieks, laughter and cries of jubilation welled from the crowd.
>
> —*Los Angeles Times,* October 23, 1944, reporting on the release of the Sleepy Lagoon defendants after their convictions were overturned

When the Sleepy Lagoon trial wrapped up in January 1943 with the conviction and sentencing of all seventeen Mexican-American defendants, most Angelenos and residents of California assumed that the whole affair was over. With the verdicts rendered and the defendants shipped off to San Quentin prison, the state's newspapers, radio stations, law enforcement agencies, and citizenry put the story behind them. They turned their attention to the ongoing war against Nazi Germany and Japan, as well as other news stories around the city, state, and country.

The leaders of the Sleepy Lagoon Defense Committee (SLDC), though, were not ready to call it quits. They believed that the convictions amounted to a clear miscarriage of justice. Just as important, they believed that the objections and claims of judicial misconduct filed by defense attorney George Shibley during the Sleepy Lagoon trial gave the SLDC a good opportunity to get the convictions overturned on appeal. Encouraged by these considerations, the SLDC and a small group of dedicated allies began raising money to finance an appeal.

Answering the Call for Justice

The first step for the SLDC was to rally public support for the so-called 38th Street Boys, the seventeen young men who had been convicted of various charges related to the death of José Díaz. To that end, SLDC chairman Carey McWilliams and executive secretary Alice Greenfield worked tirelessly to publicize the case. They knew that if they could not convince other citizens that the Sleepy Lagoon trial had been a sham, the SLDC would never be able to raise enough money to pay attorneys to mount an appeal.

In the weeks following the boys' imprisonment at San Quentin, both McWilliams and Greenfield provided vital leadership to the cause. McWilliams worked with SLDC allies to craft an effective strategy for publicizing the case to Mexican-American communities and civil rights organizations. He also personally delivered several eloquent speeches on behalf of the 38th Street Boys to labor and community groups that were seen as potentially sympathetic to the youth.

Greenfield, meanwhile, published a regular SLDC newsletter, coordinated the group's daily operations, and gave fundraising speeches herself. Greenfield's greatest contribution, however, might have been the friendships she cultivated with Henry "Hank" Leyvas and the rest of the imprisoned 38th Street Boys. Several of the boys adopted her as a favorite pen pal, and her visits to San Quentin every six weeks became a major highlight of their dreary existences. Greenfield spent these visits reassuring the inmates that they had not been forgotten. "While she remembers a range of responses to her visits, from suspicion to appreciation, she quickly realized that she had become the lifeline between them and all efforts on the outside to have them released," according to one account of the Sleepy Lagoon trial. "With many of them, she forged lasting friendships and with Hank Leyvas … an innocent infatuation."[1]

McWilliams and Greenfield were joined by a wide array of other activists. Some of these men and women formally joined the SLDC, while others established informal partnerships between their organizations and the SLDC. These allies included La Rue McCormick, the Communist activist who had been instrumental in establishing the organization that became the SLDC; labor leader Luisa Moreno; civil rights activist Josefina Fierro de Bright; SLDC treasurer Harry Braverman, a grand jury member in the case who had opposed the initial indictment of the 38th Street Boys; Charlotta Bass, who published the *California Eagle*, Los Angeles's only daily black-owned newspaper; and labor organizer Humberto "Bert" Corona and his son Frank.

In addition to these veteran labor and civil rights activists, the SLDC was greatly aided by two Sleepy Lagoon family members. Hank Leyvas's younger sister, Lupe, and Bobby Telles's mother, Margaret, both became deeply involved

Lupe Leyvas (center) talks with actor J. Edward Bromberg (left) and singer and actor Dooley Wilson during a Hollywood fundraiser for the Sleepy Lagoon Defense Committee (SLDC).

in SLDC fundraising activities. In October 1943, for example, Greenfield related how Lupe Leyvas outshone McWilliams and other SLDC speakers at a fundraising event in Hollywood. "The speaker who got the biggest hand of the evening was Lupe Leyvas," she wrote. "She only spoke for a few minutes, but she was as beautiful and charming as ever, and went over big with the crowd.... [She is] a wonderful emissary of goodwill."[2]

Working together, these crusaders were able to convince a wide array of organizations to join the fight to free the 38th Street Boys. These groups ranged from Hispanic organizations like Las Madres del Soldado Hispano-Americano (Mothers of Hispanic-American Servicemen) and the Coordinating Council for Latin American Youth (CCLAY) to labor unions such as the United Auto Workers, Brotherhood of Sleeping Car Porters, International Longshoremen's and Warehousemen's Union, and other affiliates of the powerful Congress of Industrial Organizations (CIO). The coalition was further strengthened by constitutional rights advocates and representatives from Communist groups and "left-wing" (liberal) churches, synagogues, newspapers, and magazines.

Rallying Public Support for the 38th Street Boys

The Sleepy Lagoon Defense Committee and its allies sought to rally public support to their cause by embracing two distinct but interrelated arguments. The first point of emphasis was that the actual trial had been deeply marred by the hostility and unprofessional conduct of Charles William Fricke, the judge who had presided over the Sleepy Lagoon case. According to critics, Fricke's attitude toward the defendants reflected longstanding white racist attitudes toward Mexican Americans in Los Angeles, the state of California, and the entire country. Fricke's conduct, insisted McWilliams and the SLDC, made it impossible for the 38th Street Boys to receive a fair trial.

The second argument that the SLDC made again and again was that the convictions of the 38th Street Boys signaled that the U.S. war effort, which depended on unity of purpose, was being actively undermined by Nazi agents and fascist sympathizers operating in America. The organization reminded Angelenos that when dictator Adolf Hitler and his Nazi Party built their fascist regime in Germany, one of their first priorities was to attack Jews and other minority "enemies" within their country. SLDC representatives asserted that the United States was following the same path.

The SLDC also argued that the hostile attitudes of white public officials and Anglo-controlled major newspapers toward Mexican Americans, African Americans, Jews, Communists, and other minority groups in Los Angeles and other U.S. cities placed America in grave peril. The group and its allies claimed that by increasing distrust and suspicion between America's different ethnic, religious, and political groups, people like Edward Duran Ayres and William Randolph Hearst were acting as a sort of "Fifth Column"—a term used to describe

Letters from San Quentin

During their twenty-one months in prison, the 38th Street Boys frequently wrote letters to family members and supporters like Alice Greenfield of the Sleepy Lagoon Defense Committee. These notes revealed the full range of emotions that they experienced in San Quentin during the long appeal of their convictions, including hopefulness, anger, despair, and wistful desires for reminders of the outside world. Here are excerpts from five of their letters:

> "It makes me feel good to know that the people are trying to help us."
>
> —Henry Ynostroza to Alice Greenfield

> "I thought maybe you could get me a picture of some chick! I don't care if it is a picture of Frankenstein's mama, just so I can have one to put in my awfully bare album."
>
> —Victor "Bobby" Thompson to Alice Greenfield

> "Seriously, I am serving a long, long, time for wearing a [zoot] suit like that."
>
> —José "Chepe" Ruíz

> "If the jury or the judge had been at the scene of the crime to witness what really happened, we would have never been convicted. I say this because I know."
>
> —Ysmael "Smiles" Parra

> "Did you ever make a castle out of sand or mud when you were a very small girl in pigtails and took much pain and trouble to erect it, and all of a sudden a bigger kid came over and destroyed it for you? Well my feelings are somewhat similar."
>
> —Henry "Hank" Leyvas to Alice Greenfield

Sources:

Lagoon Defense Committee Records. *Calisphere.* Retrieved from content.cdlib.org/ark:/13030/hb1x0nb4hp/?query=henry%20leyvas&brand=calisphere.

"Primary Sources." *The American Experience: Zoot Suit Riots,* 2002. Retrieved from www.pbs.org/wgbh/amex/zoot/eng_filmmore/ps.html.

"During the riots, the press, the police, the officialdom, and the dominant control groups of Los Angeles were caught with the bombs of prejudice in their hands," asserted journalist Carey McWilliams.

any group that secretly works to undermine a nation's solidarity from within. McWilliams, Greenfield, Fierro de Bright, and other prominent activists repeatedly warned that if the United States failed to withstand such efforts to divide Americans against one another, wartime morale in the United States would suffer horrible damage and the forces of fascism would be further strengthened. Labor organizer Harry Bridges even went so far as to describe discrimination in America as "Hitler's secret weapon."[3]

Not everyone was convinced by these arguments, of course. Hearst, Mayor Fletcher Bowron, and other powerful white Angelenos ridiculed these conspiracy theories, and the SLDC was repeatedly accused of being nothing more than a Communist organization that was itself devoted to undermining American democracy. This charge resonated with white Californian readers who did not want to confront any questions about the guilt of the 38th Street defendants. A significant segment of Los Angeles's Hispanic community (including *La Opinión*, the city's only Spanish-language daily paper) remained skeptical about the worthiness of SLDC's crusade as well. Older Mexican Americans, in particular, were reluctant to donate time or money to the cause. Many of them still viewed the 38th Street Boys as symbols of a zoot-suit culture that had filled them with anger or embarrassment.

Nonetheless, the SLDC persevered in its fight to swing public opinion to its side. The activists pressed their case in speeches, pamphlets, and books such as *The Sleepy Lagoon Case* (which featured a foreword by famous actor and director Orson Welles) and *The Sleepy Lagoon Mystery* (written by Hollywood screenwriter Guy Endore), and they organized all kinds of fundraising events. Their efforts had only limited success, however, until the Zoot Suit Riots swept through Los Angeles in early June 1943. In the wake of that week-long spree of mob violence and anarchy, it became harder to dismiss the SLDC's warnings about the dangers that discrimination posed to American democracy.

The SLDC sensed the change. By August 1943 one SLDC volunteer reported that he was having trouble keeping up with demand for *The Sleepy Lagoon Mystery* from Hispanic workers down at the L.A. shipyards. "They are very glad to get it," he said. "A lot of them are learning for the first time what the Sleepy Lagoon case means to *them*. They are learning the real meaning of the newspaper lies and of the riots. Once the Mexican people know that, they are that much better prepared to fight the fifth column. And the Sleepy Lagoon case is a good place to start."[4]

McWilliams, meanwhile, emphasized that he had been heartened by the support that the committee received from its very inception. He wrote that he was especially gratified by the encouragement the SLDC received from military servicemen of all different ethnic backgrounds. "We received hundreds of letters from GIs [members of the U.S. Army], from posts in Guam, New Guinea, Hawaii, the Fiji Islands, the Aleutians; in fact, from all over the world," he wrote. "Soldiers with names like Livenson, Hart, Shanahan, Hecht, Chavez, Scott, Bristol, Cavouti, and Burnham, enclosed dimes, quarters, and dollars, for the work of the committee."[5]

But McWilliams agreed that the ugliness of the Zoot Suit Riots exposed what he called "the rotten foundations" of Los Angeles's "papier-mâché façade of 'Inter-American Good Will.' ... During the riots, the press, the police, the officialdom, and the dominant control groups of Los Angeles were caught with the bombs of prejudice in their hands. One year before the riots occurred, they had been warned of the danger of an explosion. The riots were not an unexpected rupture in Anglo-Hispano relations but the logical end-product of a hundred years of neglect and discrimination."[6]

Walking Out of San Quentin

The Sleepy Lagoon Defense Committee's relentless fundraising efforts enabled the group and its allies to hire noted attorney Ben Margolis to file an appeal of the Sleepy Lagoon convictions and sentences handed down by Fricke back in January 1943. In November 1943 Margolis submitted an almost 600-page brief to the Second District Court of Appeals on behalf of the 38th Street Boys. According to his brief, the Sleepy Lagoon trial had been such a legal disaster that the court had no choice but to overturn all seventeen convictions and release all twelve of the young men who remained incarcerated in San Quentin (five of the defendants were convicted of less serious charges; they spent so much time in jail before and during the trial that they had fulfilled their sentences by the time they were handed down).

In May 1944 the Second Court of Appeals began hearing formal arguments in the case. The prosecution defended the convictions as justifiable and appropriate, but Margolis attacked the Sleepy Lagoon proceedings on a wide range of fronts. He asserted that Fricke had failed to defend the basic legal rights of

The 38th Street Boys celebrate with friends and family after hearing of their release from prison.

the defendants, such as their right to free consultations with their attorneys. He also accused the judge of establishing biased courtroom rules that unfairly tainted the defendants in the eyes of the jurors—such as his decree that the defendants could not shower, change clothes, or get haircuts in the opening weeks of the trial. Finally, Margolis argued that the prosecutors had failed to prove that there had been any conspiracy on the part of the 38th Street Boys to murder José Díaz, even though Fricke had allowed them to use evidence that should have been declared inadmissible.

On October 2, 1944, the Second Court of Appeals unanimously reversed the convictions in *People v. Zammora* and set aside the sentences. The three-judge panel agreed with Margolis's claims that the constitutional rights of the defendants had been repeatedly violated during the trial. The court also stated that it was "impossible to ascertain with the slightest degree of certainty what occurred" at the Williams Ranch on the night that Díaz died. This rebuke convinced the authorities to dismiss all charges against Leyvas and the other young men.

On the morning of October 23, 1944, Leyvas and the other Sleepy Lagoon defendants who had spent most of the previous two years at San Quentin were finally released. They were brought into a Los Angeles Superior Court courtroom, where Judge Clement D. Nye formally dismissed all charges against them. They then exited the courtroom, where they were mobbed by friends, family, and activists who had toiled on their behalf for the previous two years. "The atmosphere was electric with excitement as the liberated men were besieged by well-wishers who enthusiastically pumped their hands and slapped their backs," reported the *Los Angeles Times*. "Tears flowed unashamedly."[7]

The release of the Sleepy Lagoon defendants was a devastating setback for the family of José Díaz. Since then, however, information has trickled out that has strengthened the 38th Street Boys' claims that they had nothing to do with Díaz's death. In January 1991 a cancer-stricken elderly woman named Lorena Encinas who had grown up in the 38th Street neighborhood during the time of the Sleepy Lagoon case delivered a shocking deathbed confession to her children. She told them that back in 1942, her younger brother Louis had admitted that he was part of the Downey group that had attended the party at the Williams Ranch on the night that Díaz was attacked. Louis also confessed that after he and his friends were kicked out of the party, several of them "jumped" another young man who left the party a short time later. Both Lorena and Louis were convinced that the victim of the mugging was Díaz, but Lorena kept her brother's secret even after he committed suicide during a failed bank robbery in 1971. Sleepy Lagoon scholars such as Eduardo Obregón Pagán, however, have expressed skepticism about the Encinas story, saying that some of its elements do not match up with the existing evidence.[8]

Although the identity of Díaz's killer or killers remains shrouded in mystery, *People v. Zammora* continues to be justifiably celebrated as a landmark event in America's judicial history. As scholar Frank Bajaras wrote, the Sleepy Lagoon trial became a question of whether Mexican Americans and other minority groups had "the right to fair and equal justice before the law. In this sense the case was much larger than the young men themselves, most of whom would never win a citizen of the year award in any event. The issue was not their char-

Two Sleepy Lagoon defendants, Henry Leyvas and Gus Zamora, celebrate with family and supporters after their release from jail on October 29, 1944. Pictured left to right are Mrs. Lupe Leyvas, Saferino Leyvas, Henry Leyvas, Alice Greenfield, Gus Zamora, and Ruth Amparay.

acter, but whether the constitutional protections of the United States would prevail over blatant injustice during a time of war against fascism."[9]

Coming Home from the War

When the Sleepy Lagoon defendants gained their freedom, many Hispanics in Los Angeles and across the West reacted with a kind of dazed amazement. Discrimination, disappointment, and injustice had become so deeply interwoven into the fabric of their lives that they had not truly believed that the SLDC campaign could ever succeed. The release of the 38th Street Boys gave many Mexican Americans hope that maybe the United States really was learning to confront—and even overcome—its longstanding problems with race-based discrimination and prejudice.

"The riots were not an unexpected rupture in Anglo-Hispano relations but the logical end-product of a hundred years of neglect and discrimination," declared Carey McWilliams.

Less than two years later, the United States and its allies defeated Germany and Japan to bring World War II to an end. American servicemen poured back into the United States and returned to their civilian lives. Among the millions of veterans who came home in triumph were hundreds of thousands of servicemen of Mexican ancestry. Many of these war veterans were not satisfied to merely *hope* that the United States was becoming more accepting of people of Mexican descent. Instead, they showed a willingness to *demand* equal treatment in America's courtrooms, factories, schools, and other public facilities. And they displayed a newfound determination to make that world a reality.

These heightened expectations were a direct result of the wartime experiences of the estimated 250,000-500,000 Hispanic Americans who served in the U.S. armed forces during the conflict. (The exact number is impossible to determine since Hispanics were classified as white by the military. They served side-by-side with whites, unlike African-American soldiers, marines, airmen, and sailors, who were diverted into segregated units.) In addition, about 53,000 men from Puerto Rico served in the U.S. armed forces from 1940 to 1946. All told, people of Latino heritage accounted for 2.5 to 5 percent of all Americans who served in World War II.

Hispanic Americans served with great distinction in the war. Thirteen Hispanic servicemen earned the prestigious Medal of Honor, the highest decoration that the U.S. government can bestow on a member of the armed forces: Lucian Adams, Rudolph B. Dávila, Marcario García, Harold Gonsalves, David M. Gonzáles, Silvestre S. Herrera, José M. López, Joe P. Martínez, Manuel Pérez Jr., Cleto Rodríguez, Alejandro R. Ruiz, José F. Valdez, and Ysmael R. Villegas. Hispanic servicemen also were deeply involved in some of the most harrowing events of the war, including the 1942 Bataan Death March to Japanese prison camps in the Philippines and the June 1944 "D-Day" landing at Normandy.

Hispanics accounted for a disproportionate share of wartime draftees in many parts of the country, and Los Angeles was no exception. This relatively high draft rate was partly attributable to a legal system that allowed young Mexican Americans who ran afoul of the law to choose between prison and induction into military service. Hispanics also accounted for a disproportionate share of the city's military deaths. By the end of the war, in fact, Mexican Americans made up 20 percent of Angelenos killed in action, even though they only accounted for about 10 percent of the city's population.[10]

Seeking Full Acceptance

Many different aspects of Hispanics' wartime experiences contributed to their determination to seek full acceptance when they returned to the United States. For one thing, they knew that many white servicemen had come to appreciate the grit, bravery, and patriotism of Hispanic Americans because they had witnessed it firsthand in countless bloody skirmishes and major battles. Thousands of Hispanics who served in the military found that the racial bias they experienced on a daily basis in civilian life was absent or greatly reduced in the U.S. armed forces (see "From the Barrio to a German POW Camp—and Back," p. 185). Mexican Americans and Puerto Ricans who fought in World War II also returned home with greater self-confidence and a firmer conviction that they and their families deserved to be treated with respect. "These veterans refused to accept the blatant anti-Hispanic segregation that had been the rule for generations, especially in the Southwest,"[11] wrote historian Juan Gonzalez.

World War II had given "Mexican Americans the chance to serve as commissioned and noncommissioned officers," explained scholar Earl Shorris. "Men who had commanded Anglo troops in battle did not cringe before them in civilian life.... Sergeants and captains and buck privates turned into professional men and entrepreneurs; the vets no longer felt like intruders in a strange country. They were Americans, men who had fought for *their* country."[12] Arthur Muñoz, a Los Angeles native who served in the Marines during World War II, offered a similar assessment. "We fought as Americans, not Mexican Americans,"[13] he said.

Hispanic World War II veterans also were fully eligible for a wide range of benefits that the federal government provided to men who had served their country in wartime (in both combat and noncombat capacities). These benefits, which were introduced in the 1944 Servicemen's Readjustment Act (better known as the GI Bill), included free college or vocational education, a full year of unemployment compensation, and access to a wide range of low-interest loans to purchase homes or open businesses. "As a veteran, you have equal rights like everybody else, so it gave Mexican Americans new opportunities to

Hispanic Americans served with distinction in all branches of the U.S. Armed Forces (including the U.S. Navy, as seen here) during World War II.

go back to school or get benefits," said Marine Carlos "Charles" Samarron, who survived two of the war's fiercest battles in the Pacific Theatre, the Battle of Guam and the Battle of Iwo Jima. "It gave us a feeling of being equal."[14]

Decline of the Zoot Suit

Some of the Hispanics—and whites, Asians, and African Americans—who had gone off to war had left zoot suits hanging in their closets. When they returned home, however, they found that the fashion craze was on the decline. The pleated and billowy pants, wide-shouldered coats, dangling key chains, wide-brimmed hats, and pointed, thick-soled shoes that had been common sights in nightclubs and on city streets in the late 1930s and early 1940s were no longer seen as the height of youthful male fashion.

Part of the decline in the popularity of the zoot suit—especially in Los Angeles and other western cities—stemmed from its strong association with the Zoot Suit Riots. For many Angelenos in particular, the zoot suit had become an unpleasant reminder of an ugly chapter in the city's history. Historians and sociologists also believe, though, that the zoot suit fell out of favor because new generations of American youth wanted to carve out their own sense of style and identity. The idea of simply copying the fashion trends of their older brothers and sisters—let alone their parents—held little appeal.

Still, zoot suits maintained a presence in the world of fashion for several years. In the 1940s and early 1950s, in fact, the zoot-suit fad spread beyond U.S. borders to Canada, Mexico, the Caribbean, and even parts of Europe. Historians say that the export of American popular music and movies, the easy migration from America to Mexico and Canada for work and tourism, and the influence of U.S. servicemen stationed overseas all played a role in the brief popularization of the zoot suit outside the United States.

Zoot-suit fashion also managed to cling to life in several of America's big cities for much of the 1950s. In places like Philadelphia, New York, and Detroit, "the style still conveyed an aura of the cool hipster, necessary wear among certain cliques or for going out at night,"[15] wrote scholar Kathy Peiss. Even in these cities, however, the zoot suit could not survive. It was gradually pushed aside by new fashion styles and definitions of "cool," and by the early 1960s the zoot suit had vanished from the downtown sidewalks and glitzy nightclubs where it had once held sway.

Notes:

[1] "People & Events: Alice McGrath (1917-2009)." In *The American Experience: Zoot Suit Riots,* 2002. Retrieved from www.pbs.org/wgbh/amex/zoot/eng_peopleevents/p_mcgrath.html.

[2] Greenfield, Alice. *The Appeal News,* October 18, 1943. Retrieved from www.unitproj.library.ucla.edu/special/sleepylagoon/sldc9.htm.

[3] Quoted in Vargas, Zaragosa. *Labor Rights Are Civil Rights: Mexican American Workers in Twentieth-Century America.* Princeton, NJ: Princeton University Press, 2005, p. 231.

[4] Barajas, Frank P. "The Defense Committees of Sleepy Lagoon: A Convergent Struggle against Fascism, 1942-1944." *Aztán: A Journal of Chicano Studies,* Spring 2006, pp. 49-50.

[5] McWilliams, Carey. *North from Mexico: The Spanish-Speaking People of the United States.* Philadelphia: Lippincott, 1949, p. 232.

[6] McWilliams, p. 257.

[7] Quoted in McWilliams, p. 231.

[8] Pagán, Eduardo Obregón. *Murder at the Sleepy Lagoon: Zoot Suits, Race, and Riot in Wartime L.A.* Chapel Hill: University of North Carolina Press, 2003, pp. 416-19.

[9] Barajas, pp. 57-58.

[10] Vargas, pp. 231-32.

[11] Gonzalez, Juan. *Harvest of Empire: A History of Latinos in America.* New York: Viking, 2000, p. 170.

[12] Shorris, Earl. *Latinos: A Biography of the People.* New York: W. W. Norton, 1992, p. 97.

[13] Menchaca, Brenda. "Arthur Muñoz." In *VOCES Oral History Project: Giving Voice to the American Latino Experience,* 2001. Retrieved from www.lib.utexas.edu/voces/template-stories-indiv.html?work_urn=urn%3Autlol%3Awwlatin.641&work_title=Mu%C3%B1oz%2C+Arthur.

[14] Despres, Cliff. "Carlos 'Charles' Guerra Samarron." In *VOCES Oral History Project: Giving Voice to the American Latino Experience,* 2001. Retrieved from www.lib.utexas.edu/voces/template-stories-indiv.html?work_urn=urn%3Autlol%3Awwlatin.098&work_title=Samarron%2C+Carlos%22Charles%22Guerra.

[15] Peiss, p. 184.

Chapter Seven

LEGACY OF THE ZOOT SUIT RIOTS

> Latino patriots have served and fought in every war. They are artists, dancers, singers, poets and journalists, teachers and scientists. More and more Latinos are becoming entrepreneurs and businesspeople, contributing to the wealth and economic well-being of the nation. But they have also been characteristically humble, and have not spoken enough about their accomplishments and the contributions they have already made to the fabric of this nation.[1]
>
> —New Jersey senator Robert Menendez, 2009

As Americans of Latino heritage entered the 1950s, they had not reached any sort of consensus on what the future held for them. On the one hand, a sustained postwar economic boom gave some Mexican Americans in the West better job opportunities than ever before. This same economic upswing also attracted growing numbers of Puerto Rican immigrants to New York City. In addition, thanks to the GI Bill, thousands of Mexican-American and Puerto Rican veterans of the war were able to pursue dreams of higher education and business ownership that never would have been available to them otherwise.

The sheer number of people of Hispanic heritage in America continued to rise as well, in large part because white business interests convinced Congress to keep the wartime Bracero Program going after the war. This federally sanctioned initiative brought an estimated four million Mexican migrant agricultural workers to the United States from 1942 to 1964, when the program finally ended.

Advances in Political Representation and Civil Rights

Mexican Americans and Mexican immigrants also benefited during this period from new Hispanic groups like the American GI Forum (founded by Mexican-American World War II veterans) and the League of United Latin American Citizens (LULAC). These organizations campaigned tirelessly for equal civil rights and economic and educational opportunities in America. Meanwhile, voting registration drives in the fast-growing barrios of Los Angeles and San Antonio, Texas, resulted in the historic election of Hispanic representatives to the city councils. World War II veteran Edward Roybal (see Roybal biography, p. 145) won election to the L.A. City Council in 1949. He was followed four years later by Henry B. Gonzalez, another veteran, in San Antonio. They became the first Hispanic councilmen in their respective cities since the mid-nineteenth century (see "New Hispanic Hopes and Dreams in the Post-World War II Era," p. 180). In the early 1960s both Roybal and Gonzalez made successful runs for Congress, making Roybal the first Latino congressman from California since 1879 and Gonzalez the first Latino congressman from Texas in its entire history. Both men served with distinction in the U.S. House of Representatives for over a quarter-century.

Other signs of progress for Latinos came out of the nation's statehouses and courts. In 1947 California governor Earl Warren signed a bill (drafted in part by Hispanic businessman and community activist Manuel Ruíz Jr. of Los Angeles) that desegregated the state's public schools. Over the next few years, several poll taxes and other discriminatory measures that had been imposed in Texas to repress the black and Hispanic vote were struck down as illegal. Then, in 1954, the U.S. Supreme Court—now led by Chief Justice Earl Warren, the former California governor—issued two landmark rulings that sent shock waves across the country.

On May 3, the Court found in *Hernandez v. State of Texas* that Mexican Americans were a "distinct class" that had the right to protection from discrimination (see "A Landmark Legal Decision for Mexican Americans," p. 188). The Court's unanimous decision in the case came in response to the discovery that Jackson County, Texas, had systematically excluded Hispanics from serving as jurors for the previous twenty-five years, even though they accounted for 14 percent of the county's population.

Two weeks later, on May 17, the Supreme Court issued its famous *Brown v. Board of Education* decision, which outlawed school segregation across the United States. The Warren Court's unanimous ruling against the "separate but

In 1949 Edward R. Roybal (left) became the first Latino councilman for Los Angeles since the nineteenth century. He is seen here in a 1953 meeting with a local minister.

equal" doctrine that southern whites had long used to keep African-American students out of white schools was a civil rights milestone for black Americans, but it was a triumph for Hispanic kids as well.

For several years officials in Texas tried to circumvent the *Brown* decision by grouping black children with Hispanic children, which the state technically classified as white. In 1970, though, the federal case *Cisneros v. Corpus Christi Independent School District* extended the protections of *Brown* to Mexican Americans by explicitly identifying them as a minority group that had historically suffered discriminatory treatment. The judge asserted that school districts that just grouped black and "white" Hispanic students together were not in compliance with *Brown*. In 1973 the U.S. Supreme Court affirmed this judgment in its *Keyes v. School District No. 1* decision.

Hispanic families, communities, and activists welcomed all of these positive developments. Many of them, however, grumbled that every gain seemed to come only after years of herculean effort. The memories of the 1943 Zoot Suit Riots and other ugly spasms of racial violence and discrimination against Hispanics lingered in young and old alike. Hispanics in Los Angeles and elsewhere knew that scaling the walls of racial animosity and discrimination that remained would require years of additional toil. "While some Mexican Americans secured higher positions, the majority of them suffered through regional economic contractions, and their realization of the American dream was often thwarted by Anglos and white ethnics who still perceived them not only as dark, dangerous, exotic 'others,' but also as expendable manual laborers," wrote scholar Anthony Macias. "Thus, visible gains during the period notwithstanding, Mexican-American Angelenos still experienced class insecurity and instability."[2]

The Chicano Civil Rights Movement

The 1960s ushered in important changes in Hispanic American life. This decade was one of great tumult and change in the wider American society. American families and communities clashed over U.S. involvement in the Vietnam War, cheered and condemned the African-American civil rights movement, and heatedly debated the impact of bold new styles of music, art, fashion, and literature on the nation's values and ideals.

The civil rights movement, in particular, had a major impact on Hispanic Americans and newer immigrants from Mexico and Puerto Rico. As historian Juan Gonzalez noted, the movement's success in convincing the American people and their elected representatives to pass three landmark laws—the Civil Rights Act of 1964, the Voting Rights Act of 1965, and the Fair Housing Act of 1968—"toppled the legal underpinnings of discrimination against both blacks and Hispanics."[3]

United Farm Workers president César Chávez (left) with playwright Luis Valdez.

This supercharged environment inspired many Hispanic Americans to become more politically active, and by the late 1960s a so-called "Chicano" civil rights movement was sweeping across the United States. The term Chicano had traditionally been used as a negative, demeaning term for the sons and daughters of Mexican migrant workers, but in the late 1950s and early 1960s Mexican-American youth seized it for their own use, redefining it with connotations of ethnic pride and solidarity. By the late 1960s the term had been embraced by a growing number of Hispanic men and women who were dedicated to improving their communities and securing their full constitutional rights.

The Chicano civil rights movement encompassed campaigns devoted to a wide range of issues. Activists fought to improve educational opportunities for Hispanic children and teens, end negative stereotyping of Hispanics in American news coverage and television shows, secure new rights and higher wages for Hispanic-American workers and Mexican migrants, improve living conditions in the barrios, and instill a higher sense of cultural and ethnic pride in the nation's Latino population.

The tools used by the Chicano activists included everything from mass voter-registration drives to large-scale boycotts, strikes, and protests against white-dominated businesses and industries that were viewed as hostile to Hispanic interests. Leading activists and organizations of this era included César Chávez and Dolores Huerta, founders and leaders of the United Farm Work-

A Chicano Playwright Recreates the Zoot Suit Riots for the Stage

GRAND JURY
TO ACT IN
ZOOT SUIT WAR

Actor Edward James Olmos in a scene from *Zoot Suit*.

During the Chicano civil rights movement of the 1960s and 1970s, several influential Hispanic artists and writers retold the stories of the Sleepy Lagoon Trial and the Zoot Suit Riots that had rocked Los Angeles in the early 1940s. In their retellings, though, zoot-suited Pachucos were reinterpreted as heroic figures whose ethnic pride would become a model for later generations of Chicano activists.

The most famous of these artistic reinterpretations was *Zoot Suit,* which was written by Luis Valdez. Born in 1940 in Delano, California, to migrant farm workers, Valdez became a key figure in the development of a Chicano theater movement in the American West during the 1960s and 1970s. In the mid-1970s he wrote *Zoot Suit,* which used a blend of drama and musical numbers to tell the story of the Sleepy Lagoon murder and the riots that followed. The play's themes of racial injustice and ethnic pride, however, also resonated with other ethnic minorities in the United States.

Zoot Suit opened in Los Angeles in 1978 and was an immediate smash hit. It was performed on Broadway as well, and in 1981 a film version of Valdez's play was released. The movie starred Edward James Olmos and Henry Valdez (Luis's brother), both of whom had starred in the Broadway production. Olmos repeated his theatrical performance as El Pachuco, a mythical zoot suiter. Valdez played the role of Henry Reyna, a thinly disguised version of Henry "Hank" Leyvas, the most prominent member of the 38th Street defendants in the Sleepy Lagoon trial.

Source:

Zoot Suit Discovery Guide. Retrieved from www.research.pomona.edu/zootsuit/.

ers (UFW); Vilma Martínez and the Mexican American Legal Defense and Educational Fund (MALDEF); William C. Velásquez, founder of the Southwest Voter Registration Education Project (SVREP); and the Mexican American Political Association (MAPA), a California-based organization whose early leaders included Edward Roybal and Bert Corona.

The heightened energy and activism in America's barrios in the 1960s and 1970s also sparked bursts of Hispanic-American artistic creativity. Songs, poems, novels, plays, paintings, and sculptures that celebrated Latino life and history came pouring out of the Hispanic-American community during these years. The most famous of these works was the smash hit theatrical production *Zoot Suit*. This play, written and directed by Luis Valdez, first premiered in Los Angeles in 1978 and became the first Hispanic production ever to appear on Broadway.

All of these disparate movements worked together to lift the fortunes of Latinos at the same time that their community was becoming more diverse. For most of the twentieth century, Hispanics in America had come from Mexico or, to a much lesser degree, Puerto Rico. In the 1960s and succeeding decades, however, America received a growing number of Latinos from Central America and the Caribbean. Most of these new arrivals were political and economic refugees from Cuba, the Dominican Republic, El Salvador, Nicaragua, and Guatemala.

A Mix of Encouraging and Troubling Trends

During the 1980s Latino populations in California, Texas, Florida, and several northern cities continued to swell. This growth was fueled primarily by rising levels of immigration (both legal and illegal) and higher-than-national-average birth rates in Hispanic households. The latter phenomenon has been attributed to several factors, including low Hispanic use of birth control because of Catholic teachings that reject the use of contraceptives; traditional enthusiasm for large families; and rising rates of teen and out-of-wedlock pregnancy.

This population growth gave Latinos greater political representation in major U.S. cities like Los Angeles, San Antonio, Miami, New York, Chicago, and Philadelphia than ever before. Eleven Hispanics were serving in the U.S. House of Representatives by the late 1980s as well, including the body's first Hispanic female, Cuban-born Ileana Ros-Lehtinen of Florida. (In contrast, the U.S. Senate had only three Hispanic members—all representing New Mexico—in the entire twentieth century, and none from 1977 to 2005, when Hispanic senators from Colorado and Florida took office.)

As the 1980s gave way to the 1990s, portraits of Latino-American life in the United States presented a confusing and contradictory blend of positive and negative trends. On the one hand, Hispanics were graduating from high school, attending college, establishing new businesses, buying homes, and obtaining good-paying jobs in greater numbers than ever before. Many Latino families also felt fully assimilated into American culture, even as they maintained a strong sense of ethnic pride. Illegal immigrants from Latin America, meanwhile, took advantage when Washington devised pathways for them to become legal residents during these decades. In 1986, for example, President Ronald Reagan signed the Immigration Reform and Control Act, which extended "amnesty" (legal pardons) to qualified illegal immigrants who wanted to become legal citizens of the United States. Of the three million illegal immigrants who eventually became legal U.S. residents under the legislation, 2.6 million were from Latin America.[4]

These positive trends, however, were obscured by other trends that were cause for great concern. Latino communities struggled with the highest rates of teen pregnancy and high school dropouts, a surge in the percentage of male Latinos in prison, and escalating violence, drug dealing, and other criminal activity from youth gangs. All of these factors were cited as contributors to—and outgrowths of—stubbornly high rates of poverty in Latino-American households.

Hispanic Americans in the Twenty-First Century

All of these social and economic problems have continued to trouble Hispanic-American communities in the early twenty-first century. In terms of overall rates of educational attainment, household income, and other important indicators of family and community health, Latinos lag far behind white and Asian Americans, and they have fallen behind African Americans in some areas as well. According to the Pew Hispanic Center, for instance, more than 37 percent of American children living in poverty in the United States are Latino (a total of 6.1 million kids), even though Hispanics account for only 16 percent of the total U.S. population.[5]

Some scholars believe that these statistics are misleading and do not tell the whole story. In 2011, for example, a study published in the *Journal of Labor Economics* found that the parents of more than 25 percent of third-generation children with Mexican ancestry do not even identify their children as Latino on Census forms. Most of the Latinos who make this decision are highly educated, economically secure, and fluent in English, but they have also coupled

Hispanic-American Statistical Trends, 2010

The statistical data presented here and on the following pages, tabulated by the Pew Hispanic Center, provide insights into the socioeconomic challenges facing Hispanic-American families and communities in the twenty-first century.

STATISTICAL PORTRAIT OF HISPANICS IN THE UNITED STATES, 2010

Educational Attainment, by Race and Ethnicity: 2010

Universe: 2010 resident population ages 25 and older

	Less than 9th grade	9th to 12th grade	High school graduate	Some college	College graduate	Total
Hispanic	6,131,310	4,174,618	7,215,592	6,225,777	3,588,593	27,335,890
Native born	953,270	1,546,931	3,437,299	3,861,097	2,048,199	11,846,796
Foreign born	5,178,040	2,627,687	3,778,293	2,364,680	1,540,394	15,489,094
White alone, not Hispanic	4,069,662	8,896,410	40,902,298	41,904,683	43,924,341	139,697,394
Black alone, not Hispanic	1,176,878	2,941,409	7,338,359	7,481,968	4,142,690	23,081,304
Asian alone, not Hispanic	836,191	580,090	1,587,467	1,921,373	4,956,912	9,882,033
Other, not Hispanic	215,719	410,283	1,167,807	1,495,770	1,059,929	4,349,508
Total	**12,429,760**	**17,002,810**	**58,211,523**	**59,029,571**	**57,672,465**	**204,346,129**
PERCENT DISTRIBUTION						
Hispanic	22.4	15.3	26.4	22.8	13.1	100.0
Native born	8.0	13.1	29.0	32.6	17.3	100.0
Foreign born	33.4	17.0	24.4	15.3	9.9	100.0
White alone, not Hispanic	2.9	6.4	29.3	30.0	31.4	100.0
Black alone, not Hispanic	5.1	12.7	31.8	32.4	17.9	100.0
Asian alone, not Hispanic	8.5	5.9	16.1	19.4	50.2	100.0
Other, not Hispanic	5.0	9.4	26.8	34.4	24.4	100.0
All	**6.1**	**8.3**	**28.5**	**28.9**	**28.2**	**100.0**

Notes: "Some college" includes persons who have attained an associate's degree; "college graduate" includes persons who have attained a bachelor's degree. "Other, not Hispanic" includes persons reporting single races not listed separately and persons reporting more than one race.

Source: Pew Hispanic Center tabulations of 2010 American Community Survey (1% IPUMS)

PEW HISPANIC CENTER

PewResearchCenter

STATISTICAL PORTRAIT OF HISPANICS IN THE UNITED STATES, 2010

Poverty, by Age, Race and Ethnicity: 2010

Universe: 2010 household population

	PERSONS IN POVERTY			
	Younger than 18	18 to 64	65 and older	Total
Hispanic	5,518,326	6,267,930	512,940	12,299,196
Native born	4,970,026	2,584,745	192,779	7,747,550
Foreign born	548,300	3,683,185	320,161	4,551,646
White alone, not Hispanic	5,216,671	13,045,458	2,180,258	20,442,387
Black alone, not Hispanic	3,910,759	5,273,995	593,477	9,778,231
Asian alone, not Hispanic	400,576	1,166,744	178,113	1,745,433
Other, not Hispanic	869,741	917,370	70,113	1,857,224
Total	**15,916,073**	**26,671,497**	**3,534,901**	**46,122,471**

	POVERTY RATE (%)			
	Younger than 18	18 to 64	65 and older	Total
Hispanic	32.4	20.9	18.7	24.7
Native born	31.7	18.1	15.7	24.8
Foreign born	39.9	23.5	21.0	24.5
White alone, not Hispanic	13.2	10.7	7.0	10.6
Black alone, not Hispanic	38.1	23.1	18.3	26.9
Asian alone, not Hispanic	12.7	12.0	13.0	12.2
Other, not Hispanic	23.6	19.5	13.4	20.8
All	**21.6**	**14.1**	**9.0**	**15.3**

Notes: Due to the way in which the IPUMS adjusts annual incomes, these data will differ from those that might be provided by the U.S. Census Bureau. "Other, not Hispanic" includes persons reporting single races not listed separately and persons reporting more than one race.

Source: Pew Hispanic Center tabulations of 2010 American Community Survey (1% IPUMS)

PEW HISPANIC CENTER PewResearchCenter

with non-Hispanic whites to produce their children. Their Census choices have created a situation in which many people of Mexican descent who are actually thriving in the United States are not showing up in statistics designed to track Latino economic and social progress across generations.[6]

Even taking such studies into account, however, conservative and liberal observers alike agree that the socioeconomic status of Latino Americans has to be improved, not only for the sake of future generations of Latino children, but

STATISTICAL PORTRAIT OF HISPANICS IN THE UNITED STATES, 2010

Population Change, by Race and Ethnicity: 2000 and 2010

Universe: 2000 and 2010 resident population

	2010 population	2000 population	Change, 2000-2010	Percent change, 2000-2010	Share of total change (%)
Hispanic	50,729,570	35,204,480	15,525,090	44.1	55.6
Native born	31,912,465	21,072,230	10,840,235	51.4	38.8
Foreign born	18,817,105	14,132,250	4,684,855	33.2	16.8
White alone, not Hispanic	196,931,448	194,527,123	2,404,325	1.2	8.6
Black alone, not Hispanic	37,936,978	33,706,554	4,230,424	12.6	15.1
Asian alone, not Hispanic	14,558,242	10,088,521	4,469,721	44.3	16.0
Other, not Hispanic	9,193,451	7,895,228	1,298,223	16.4	4.6
Total	**309,349,689**	**281,421,906**	**27,927,783**	**9.9**	**100.0**

Note: "Other, not Hispanic" includes persons reporting single races not listed separately and persons reporting more than one race.

Source: Pew Hispanic Center tabulations of 2000 Census (5% IPUMS) and 2010 American Community Survey (1% IPUMS)

PEW HISPANIC CENTER PewResearchCenter

also to ensure the health and vitality of California, Texas, and other states with large Hispanic populations. After all, demographic experts believe that if current trends hold steady, Hispanics will account for one-third of the total U.S. population by 2050.

Although liberals and conservatives diagnose the same social problems, however, they usually propose solutions that are unacceptable to the other side. This divide is apparent in the realm of illegal immigration, for example. In 2010 the U.S. government estimated that about 11.2 million unauthorized immigrants were living and working in the United States. The majority of these illegal aliens are from Mexico, where poverty and crime levels are far higher than in America. As a consequence, tens of thousands of desperate Mexicans decide every year that even a life of struggle and uncertainty in the United States is better than one of certain misery in their native land. Conservatives have, in general, supported a variety of measures that they say will halt this flow, which they believe contributes to wider societal problems such as poverty, crime, unemployment among U.S. citizens, and "runaway" government spending on social programs for the poor. Con-

Who Is a "Typical" Latino American?

The U.S. Census categorizes people by race, which is defined by a set of common physical traits, but it also recognizes that people of Hispanic, Latino, or Spanish origin may be of any race. The majority of Hispanics classify themselves as white. *New York Times* journalist Miraya Navarro notes, however, that "many Latinos say they are too racially mixed to settle on one of the government-sanctioned standard races—white, black, American Indian, Alaska native, native Hawaiian, and a collection of Asian and Pacific Island backgrounds. Some regard white or black as separate demographic groups from Latino. Still others say Latinos are already the equivalent of another race in this country, defined by a shared set of challenges." As a result, Navarro noted, "Latinos tend to identify themselves more by their ethnicity, meaning a shared set of cultural traits, like language or customs." In other words, they define themselves primarily as people of Cuban, Mexican, Salvadoran, Puerto Rican, Dominican, or other descent and only secondarily as "Latinos" or "Hispanics."

Other Latinos, meanwhile, claim that even country classifications cannot adequately summarize their complex family histories. "An overwhelming majority of [non-Mexican Latinos] aren't solely of Spanish, black, or native origin," writes journalist and filmmaker Raquel Cepeda. "We're all of the above and then some (some of our ancestors migrated from Asian, Middle Eastern, and an array of European countries).... Take me, for example; I'm a first-generation American, the product of Dominican parents.... [but] my family is made up of a rainbow coalition of racial chameleons. Recently, I was told that my maternal grandmother's own abuela [grandma] was Vietnamese; my maternal great-great-grandfather was Haitian; somewhere on my paternal side, we're supposedly Sephardic [Jews]."

Sources:

Cepeda, Raquel. "But What's a Latino?" *CNN.com,* October 22, 2009. Retrieved from www.cnn.com/2009/LIVING/10/22/cepeda.latino.census/index.html.

Navarro, Miraya. "For Many Latinos, Racial Identity Is More Culture Than Color." *New York Times,* January 14, 2012. Retrieved from www.nytimes.com/2012/01/14/us/for-many-latinos-race-is-more-culture-than-color.html?_r=1&pagewanted=all.

STATISTICAL PORTRAIT OF HISPANICS IN THE UNITED STATES, 2010

Detailed Hispanic Origin: 2010

Hispanic populations are listed in descending order of population size

Universe: 2010 Hispanic resident population

	Number	Percent
Mexican	32,915,983	64.9
Puerto Rican	4,682,531	9.2
Cuban	1,883,599	3.7
Salvadoran	1,827,290	3.6
All Other Spanish/Hispanic/Latino	1,567,169	3.1
Dominican	1,509,060	3.0
Guatemalan	1,107,859	2.2
Colombian	972,334	1.9
Honduran	730,954	1.4
Spaniard	707,135	1.4
Ecuadorian	664,781	1.3
Peruvian	609,360	1.2
Nicaraguan	376,747	0.7
Argentinean	239,509	0.5
Venezuelan	238,779	0.5
Panamanian	174,458	0.3
Chilean	139,480	0.3
Costa Rican	127,575	0.3
Bolivian	112,028	0.2
Uruguayan	63,784	0.1
Other Central American	31,260	0.1
Other South American	26,594	0.1
Paraguayan	21,301	0.0
Total	**50,729,570**	**100.0**

Source: Pew Hispanic Center tabulations of 2010 American Community Survey (1% IPUMS)

PEW HISPANIC CENTER

PewResearchCenter

Latino American spectators at a East Los Angeles Mexican independence parade.

servative media personalities and political leaders have supported major new investments in border security and state laws that emphasize identification and deportation of undocumented immigrants and curtailment of their rights.

Several such laws passed in states like Arizona, Colorado, and Alabama in 2010 and 2011 have been defended by supporters as long overdue—and condemned by opponents as cruel, shortsighted, and racially motivated. Liberal policymakers, media figures, and organizations assert that a better approach would be to 1) adopt policies that provide ways for undocumented immigrants of good character to obtain U.S. citizenship, and 2) make greater investment in programs that lift the economic and educational fortunes of immigrants. Conservatives say that such proposals are too expensive and ignore the fact that illegal aliens are in America in clear violation of established U.S. law.

Rising Political Power

As the debate over immigration reform has raged inconclusively, Latino-American population growth has continued to accelerate. From 2000 to

2010, Hispanics accounted for more than half of the nation's total population growth, and they now account for one in four American newborns. In California, Arizona, New Mexico, Texas, Florida, New York, Colorado, and other states with large concentrations of Latinos, they have achieved a level of political, economic, and cultural influence that they have never had before (see "Honoring the Heritage and Contributions of Hispanic Americans," p. 193). The city that was the site of the anti-Hispanic Zoot Suit Riots, for example, elected a Latino mayor, Antonio Villaraigosa, in 2005. The enhanced visibility of Latinos can be seen at the national level, too. In August 2009 Sonia Sotomayor became the first Hispanic justice in the history of the U.S. Supreme Court, and as of 2012 the U.S. Congress was home to 24 Latino representatives and two Latino senators.

Some whites and African Americans have expressed concern—and even alarm—about the fast-rising number of people of Hispanic heritage in American society. Ronald Bailey of *Reason* magazine, though, believes that concerns that whites will be a minority in the United States are "silly and nearly meaningless" due to natural assimilation and rising rates of intermarriage between people of different ethnic groups. "By 2050, just as the earlier waves of Irish, Italian, Jewish, and Polish immigrants were assimilated, so too will today's Hispanic immigrants and their descendants be. For all intents and purposes, Hispanics will become as 'white' as Irish, Italians, Jews, and Poles [who were once regarded as non-Anglos].... It is my hope and belief that Americans of whatever ancestry living in 2050 will look back and wonder why ever did anyone care about the ethnic makeup of the American population. America is an ideal, not a tribe."[7]

Hispanic senator Robert Menendez of New Jersey offers a similarly optimistic take on the ability of Latino Americans to assimilate and contribute to the vitality of the United States. He acknowledges, though, that Hispanics also face daunting challenges in the years ahead. "Millions of Latinos are graduating into the middle class," he wrote. "More Latino children are going to colleges and universities than ever before. Latinos are increasingly serving in public office and in key areas of the economy. But, at the same time, despite this progress in education, too many Latino children are dropping out of school. Too many families are struggling to make ends meet.... These are the realities, some we can justifiably be proud of. Others we must honestly confront and address if we are to succeed together as a nation, achieve our full potential, and bring the next generation along."[8]

Notes:

[1] Menendez, Robert. "Latinos Have Made It, but There's Still Work to Be Done." *CNN: Latino in America,* October 19, 2009. Retrieved from www.cnn.com/2009/LIVING/10/19/menendez.latino.america/index.html.

[2] Macias, Anthony. *Mexican American Mojo: Popular Music, Dance, and Urban Culture in Los Angeles, 1935-1968.* Durham, NC: Duke University Press, 2008, p. 5.

[3] Gonzalez, Juan. *Harvest of Empire: A History of Latinos in America.* New York: Viking, 2000, p. 172.

[4] Gonzalez, p. 186.

[5] Lopez, Mark Hugo, and Gabriel Velasco. "Childhood Poverty Among Hispanics Sets Record, Leads Nation." *Pew Hispanic Center,* September 28, 2011. Retrieved from www.pewhispanic.org/2011/09/28/childhood-poverty-among-hispanics-sets-record-leads-nation/.

[6] Duncan, Brian, and Stephen J. Trejo. "Intermarriage and the Intergenerational Transmission of Ethnic Identity and Human Capital for Mexican Americans." *Journal of Labor Economics,* April 2011, pp. 195-227.

[7] Bailey, Ronald. "The Silly Panic over a Minority White Nation." *Reason,* February 21, 2012. Retrieved from www.reason.com/archives/2012/02/21/white-majority-minority-2050.

[8] Menendez, "Latinos Have Made It, but There's Still Work to Be Done."

BIOGRAPHIES

Fletcher Bowron (1887-1968)

Mayor of Los Angeles during the Sleepy Lagoon Trial and Zoot Suit Riots

Fletcher Bowron was born in Poway, California, on August 13, 1887. The youngest of three sons, he followed both of his brothers to the University of California, Berkeley. After two years at Berkeley he enrolled at the University of Southern California (USC) Law School in 1909. He worked his way through school by serving as a reporter for several newspapers in San Francisco, Oakland, and Los Angeles. He passed the bar exam in 1917 to become a licensed attorney in California.

Bowron's legal career was delayed by World War I. When the United States entered the conflict in 1917, Bowron enlisted in the U.S. Army. He served in both the artillery and military intelligence divisions over the course of the next year. When the war ended in November 1918 Bowron returned home and began practicing law. In 1922 he married Irene Martin.

From Judge to Mayor

In 1923 Bowron was appointed as a deputy state corporations commissioner, a position that called for him to oversee the application of a number of important financial regulations in California. Three years later, the state's conservative governor, Friend Richardson, appointed him to a judgeship on the state's superior court. Bowron spent the next twelve years working for California in that capacity.

In 1938 Bowron was swept into the Los Angeles mayor's office by a groundswell of popular outrage with the corrupt administration of Mayor Frank Shaw. His promises to clean up city hall and reform the L.A. police department resonated with city voters, who made Shaw the first mayor of a major American city to be recalled from office. Bowron won the special election to replace Shaw, and he was sworn in on September 26, 1938.

Bowron served as mayor of Los Angeles for the next fifteen years. He won re-election four times, but he left office on June 30, 1953, after losing a bid for a fifth term. Bowron was in some ways a tremendous success as mayor. He rooted out a lot of the corruption that had been festering in the city's police department and various city agencies. In addition, he presided over a period of tremendous city growth, both in terms of economic vitality and infrastructure development. For example, he provided essential political muscle for a host of major works projects—including new highways, airports, public housing, and skyscrapers—that became important building blocks in the creation of modern-day Los Angeles. Through it all, Bowron relied heavily on what biographer Tom Sitton called his "personal integrity and ability to convey it to his constituents."[1]

Failing to Stand Up to Race-Baiting

The shakiest part of Bowron's record came in the realm of race relations. He was not a rabid racist, but he harbored many of the same stereotypical beliefs about African Americans and Mexican Americans as other white Angelenos. Time and again, he attributed the struggles of minority communities to personal failings, paying little heed to the heavy discrimination that Hispanics and blacks experienced in the city's schools, workplaces, and neighborhoods. He also supported the police department's approach to dealing with juvenile delinquent "zoot suiters." The city police emphasized punishment and intimidation over rehabilitation or community outreach programs. When minority community leaders complained that many youth—wearing zoot suits or not—were being treated as if they were guilty unless proven innocent, Bowron accused the city's blacks and Hispanics of "widespread prejudice against police officers."[2]

Bowron also lobbied heavily for the internment of Japanese Americans during World War II. On February 12, 1942, for example, Bowron delivered a radio address in which he asked, "If [Abraham] Lincoln were alive today, what would he do ... to defend the nation against the Japanese horde?" He then answered his own question, declaring that "there isn't a shadow of a doubt but that Lincoln, the mild-mannered man whose memory we regard with almost saint-like reverence, would make short work of rounding up the Japanese and putting them where they could do no harm."[3]

Bowron's response to the notorious Zoot Suit Riots, which exploded across Los Angeles for a week in June 1943, has also been heavily criticized. The mayor made little effort to intervene in the opening days of the riots, even as reports piled up that city police were contributing to the mayhem and violence. After the riots ended, Bowron steadfastly rejected any and all charges that the riots had been triggered by racial prejudice on the part of city police, military personnel, or white civilians. He insisted that the clashes could be attributed to longstanding tensions between two groups—sailors and civilians—who were young and impulsive.

Final Years as Mayor

As the years passed by, Bowron's stance toward minority rights in Los Angeles did shift somewhat. In 1944 he urged streetcar companies to end their ban on hiring black conductors, and one year later he called on the state legislature to pass a Fair Employment Practices Act. In the late 1940s he also supported reforms to end segregation in public housing. Nonetheless, his overall record on race is generally regarded as one of the weakest parts of his long tenure.

In 1953 Bowron lost his bid for another term as mayor. Undaunted, he decided to return to the world of law. In 1956 he won a six-year term as a superior court judge. He fulfilled his term, then retired from political life in 1962. By this time his wife Irene had died (in January 1961, after a long illness) and he had married his executive assistant, Albine Norton. Bowron remained active in the city's legal and political environment for the next six years. On September 11, 1968, however, he suffered a fatal heart attack and crashed into a brick wall while driving. He is remembered today as a flawed but important figure in the development of one of America's great cities.

Sources:

Alvarez, Luis. *The Power of the Zoot: Youth Culture and Resistance During World War II.* Berkeley: University of California Press, 2008.

Sitton, Tom. *Los Angeles Transformed: Fletcher Bowron's Urban Reform Revival, 1938-1953.* Albuquerque: University of New Mexico Press, 2005.

Notes:

[1] Sitton, Tom. *Los Angeles Transformed: Fletcher Bowron's Urban Reform Revival, 1938-1953.* Albuquerque: University of New Mexico Press, 2005, p. 199.

[2] Alvarez, Luis. *The Power of the Zoot: Youth Culture and Resistance During World War II.* Berkeley: University of California Press, 2008, p. 50.

[3] Quoted in Chuman, Frank F. *The Bamboo People: The Law and Japanese-Americans.* Del Mar, CA: Publisher's Inc., 1976, p 150.

José Díaz (1919-1942)

Mexican Farm Worker whose Murder Resulted in the Sleepy Lagoon Trial

José Gallardo Díaz was born on December 9, 1919, in Durango, Mexico. Four years later, he and his parents and two siblings fled to California to escape the terrible poverty and political unrest that afflicted their native country. By 1928 the family had settled outside of Los Angeles, where there was heavy demand for field laborers who would work long hours for low pay. Their home was a simple bunkhouse, one of a cluster of buildings that housed farm workers at a property known as the Williams Ranch.

Young Díaz left school after eighth grade in order to help support his family. He worked at a nearby vegetable packing plant with his brother and sister. As he grew older, Díaz acquired a reputation as a fairly soft-spoken and mild-mannered young man. Nonetheless, he joined the legions of other young black, white, and Mexican youth who began sporting zoot suits and dancing at weekend parties in the late 1930s and early 1940s.

A Fateful Birthday Party

In the summer of 1942 Díaz enlisted in the U.S. Army. This decision greatly alarmed his mother, but he thought that military service would give him an opportunity to make his mark in the world—and perhaps open the door to opportunities to be something other than a farm worker for the rest of his life. The weekend before he was scheduled to report to basic training, his mother arranged to have his portrait taken. In the photograph, which was the first and last one ever taken of Díaz, "he is dressed neatly, with hair well-combed, looking young and ambitious,"[1] according to a PBS special on the Zoot Suit Riots. That Saturday, he attended a birthday party at the Williams Ranch for Eleanor Delgadillo Coronado, a young woman whose parents worked on the property.

The party was a rowdy affair, with a lot of drinking and some fighting. Sometime after midnight Díaz left the Delgadillo house to head home. After all, he was scheduled to report for military service the next day. Eleanor Delgadillo later said she saw Díaz leaving with two boys named Luís "Cito" Vargas and Andrew Torres, but other witnesses gave conflicting information about when Díaz left.

A few minutes after Delgadillo said that she saw Díaz leave, a large group of angry young Mexican Americans from the city's 38th Street neighborhood showed up at the Delgadillo house. They were searching for the men who had attacked some members of their group at a nearby reservoir called Sleepy Lagoon. Tensions between the 38th Street folks and the partygoers quickly escalated, triggering an ugly brawl. After the 38th Street crowd finally left the ranch, the badly wounded body of Díaz was found by the side of the road. It appeared that he had been the victim of a brutal robbery. He died of his injuries shortly after he was taken to a local hospital.

A Forgotten Man

Díaz's death sparked a swift response from Los Angeles police and municipal authorities who had been warning Angelenos for years that Mexican-American youth gangs posed a rising threat. The so-called Sleepy Lagoon Murder also became a favorite topic of the city's newspapers. When prosecutors leveled murder charges against seventeen young men from the 38th Street neighborhood, the papers congratulated the authorities for finally moving against the "baby gangsters." In early 1943 all of the accused men were convicted of charges related to Díaz's murder.

Within two years, though, the Sleepy Lagoon murder trial became an embarrassment to the city. The trial had been so saturated with anti-Mexican bias and flawed rulings by the presiding judge that an appeals court overturned the convictions in October 1944. All of the 38th Street Boys were set free. Historians believe that the entire episode showed that Los Angeles law enforcement authorities and reporters became more caught up in using Díaz's death as a weapon against the city's Hispanic youth than in ensuring that Díaz's killers were brought to justice. "He was far more interesting to the public in death as a victim of gang violence than he was as the son of Mexican refugees struggling to make a place for themselves within the narrow confines prescribed by American society," wrote Eduardo Obregón Pagán. "Newspapers and court dockets dutifully noted when he was born, when he died, the medical complications that choked off his young life, but little else."[2]

Investigators declined to reopen the Díaz case after the Sleepy Lagoon defendants were freed. This was a source of great pain and sorrow to surviving family members, who never found out how—or by whose hand—he died on that August night in 1942.

Sources:

Pagán, Eduardo Obregón. *Murder at the Sleepy Lagoon: Zoot Suits, Race, and Riot in Wartime L.A.* Chapel Hill: University of North Carolina Press, 2003.

"People & Events: José Gallardo Díaz (1919-1942)." In *The American Experience: Zoot Suit Riots,* 2002. Retrieved from www.pbs.org/wgbh/amex/zoot/eng_peopleevents/p_diaz.html.

Notes:

[1] "People & Events: José Gallardo Díaz (1919-1942)." In *The American Experience: Zoot Suit Riots,* 2002. Retrieved from www.pbs.org/wgbh/amex/zoot/eng_peopleevents/p_diaz.html.

[2] Pagán, Eduardo Obregón. *Murder at the Sleepy Lagoon: Zoot Suits, Race, and Riot in Wartime L.A.* Chapel Hill: University of North Carolina Press, 2003, p. 63.

Charles William Fricke (1882-1958)
Judge Who Presided over the 1943 Sleepy Lagoon Murder Trial

Charles William Fricke was born in 1882 in Milwaukee, Wisconsin. He attended New York University, where he earned his master's degree and doctorate degree in law. Fricke then returned to Wisconsin, where he served as a district attorney and municipal judge for several years.

Fricke was a physically frail young man, though, and in 1915 he decided to move to California to escape Wisconsin's long winters. He relocated to Los Angeles, where he became a prosecutor in the city's district attorney's office. By the late 1920s he had been promoted to chief deputy. During this same period he became an accomplished textbook writer on various aspects of criminal law.

"San Quentin Fricke"

In 1927 Fricke was appointed by Governor C. C. Young to fill a vacancy on the state's Superior Court bench. "As a judge, Fricke continued along the same philosophical trajectory that he established as a prosecutor," wrote historian Eduardo Obregón Pagán. "Not only did he earn a reputation for favoring the prosecution during his twenty-five years as a judge in Los Angeles, but he also earned the nickname 'San Quentin Fricke' for having sent more people to San Quentin State Prison than any other judge in California history."[1]

During his years on the bench, Fricke also was a relentless critic of separate juvenile courts for underage lawbreakers. He saw "alternative" sentencing, such as community service, as a weak substitute for actual jail time. As a result, Fricke repeatedly sent young lawbreakers—and especially repeat offenders—to state prison rather than state forest work camps or other alternatives.

As a judge, Fricke was a prominent member of Los Angeles's white economic and political elite. Many white Angelenos became hostile to Mexican-American members of their community during the 1930s and 1940s. Prodded by overblown newspaper reports of Mexican-American juvenile delinquents and their own racist impulses, they increasingly regarded Hispanics as undesirable interlopers rather than longstanding parts of the city's economic and cultural fabric. This negative attitude toward Hispanics (and other minorities) became particularly evident among white police officers and other officials responsible for keeping public order.

The Sleepy Lagoon Trial

In 1942 Fricke drew the case of *People v. Zammora*, better known as the Sleepy Lagoon murder trial. The highly publicized case featured seventeen Mexican-American defendants from the city's 38th Street neighborhood who had been accused of involvement in the murder of a migrant farm worker named José Díaz.

People v. Zammora was the largest mass trial in the history of Los Angeles, and Fricke faced significant logistical challenges in trying so many defendants at once in his small courtroom. He ultimately decided to seat the defendants in two rows directly opposite the jury box. The defense lawyers were kept at the defense table, and Fricke refused to allow them to communicate with their clients while court was in session. This stern ruling had the effect of denying the defendants their constitutional "right to counsel"—the right to consult with the attorneys representing them in a timely fashion.

As the trial progressed, Fricke issued numerous other rulings that gave a big edge to the prosecution. One of the most momentous of these rulings came at the very beginning, when he refused to allow the defendants to change into clean clothing or cut their hair for the first month of the trial. This decision shocked the defense team, reporters from the city's black and Hispanic papers, and supporters of the so-called 38th Street Boys, but Fricke was unmoved. Many years later, scholars still point to this decision by Fricke as the clearest piece of evidence that the trial was, in the words of California historian Kevin Starr, "a farce.... [Fricke] refused to allow the young men to groom themselves and dress properly for court. Day in, day out, they sat together in their soiled clothes, their dark faces and unkempt appearance proof positive, as Judge Fricke intended, of their guilt."[2]

Fricke also became openly hostile to defense attorney George Shibley, who registered numerous objections to the court proceedings so that the defendants would have grounds to file appeals in the likely event that they were found guilty. The judge, however, accused Shibley of intentionally stalling the trial's progress out of spite. By the latter stages of the twelve-week trial, the frustrated Fricke "increasingly demeaned Shibley and the defendants in front of the jury, thereby reducing their credibility and any hope for a fair trial."[3]

To no one's surprise, the jury returned guilty verdicts for all of the Sleepy Lagoon defendants. Armed with these verdicts, Fricke imposed harsh sentences on the seventeen defendants. He imposed life sentences on the three young men who had been found guilty of first-degree murder, five-years-to-life sentences on nine more who had been found guilty of second-degree murder, and six-month-to-one-year sentences on the remaining five, who had been found guilty of assault (these five youths were released because they had already spent so much time in jail).

An Embarrassing Rebuke

The verdicts in the Sleepy Lagoon trial were immediately challenged by the Sleepy Lagoon Defense Committee (SLDC), an organization of private citizens who believed that the entire trial had been a stunning miscarriage of justice. The SLDC funded legal appeals that attacked virtually every facet of Fricke's performance. In October 1944 an appeals court sided with the SLDC and the 38th Street Boys and overturned all the convictions. The appeals court stated that the guilt of the accused had never been proven, that Fricke had displayed clear favoritism toward the prosecution, and that he had deprived the defendants of their constitutional rights.

The appeals court decision was a clear and very public rebuke of Fricke's performance on the bench, but it did not have any lasting effects on his career. He remained popular with white Anglos, who re-elected him several times. Fricke also continued to author textbooks on criminal law, and he lectured at both Loyola Law School and the Los Angeles Police Academy. Fricke remained a superior court judge in Los Angeles until his death on January 28, 1958.

Sources:

Mazón, Mauricio. *The Zoot Suit Riots: The Psychology of Symbolic Annihilation.* Austin: University of Texas Press, 1984.

Pagán, Eduardo Obregón. *Murder at the Sleepy Lagoon: Zoot Suits, Race, and Riot in Wartime L.A.* Chapel Hill: University of North Carolina Press, 2003.

Rasmussen, Cecilia. "Notorious Cases for a 'No-Nonsense' Judge." *Los Angeles Times,* August 20, 2006. Retrieved from www.articles.latimes.com/2006/aug/20/local/me-then20.

Notes:

[1] Pagán, Eduardo Obregón. *Murder at the Sleepy Lagoon: Zoot Suits, Race, and Riot in Wartime L.A.* Chapel Hill: University of North Carolina Press, 2003, p. 80.

[2] Starr, Kevin. *Embattled Dreams: California in War and Peace, 1940-1950.* New York: Oxford University Press, 2003, p. 102.

[3] "People & Events: Judge Charles Williams Fricke (1882-1958)." In *The American Experience: Zoot Suit Riots,* 2002. Retrieved from www.pbs.org/wgbh/amex/zoot/eng_peopleevents/p_fricke.html.

Alice Greenfield (1917-2009)

Civil Rights Activist and Member of the Sleepy Lagoon Defense Committee

Alice Greenfield (later Alice Greenfield McGrath) was born on April 5, 1917, to Russian Jewish immigrants in Calgary, Canada. In 1922 her family moved to Los Angeles, where she spent the rest of her childhood and adolescence. During these years she developed a strong sympathy for minority residents of the city, who were routinely subjected to hostility and discrimination from the majority white community.

After graduating from high school Greenfield worked briefly in a candy factory and as a salesperson for a local book publisher. She was also drawn to liberal political causes, however, and in the late 1930s she began volunteering her time to the Congress of Industrial Organizations (CIO) labor group.

Greenfield and the Sleepy Lagoon Trial

Greenfield's work with the CIO brought her into contact with a number of leading progressive lawyers, labor leaders, and civil rights activists in California. One of these individuals was George Shibley, who in late 1942 became the lead defense attorney in the case of *People v. Zammora*, better known in the Los Angeles press as the Sleepy Lagoon trial. The defendants in the case were seventeen young Mexican-American men accused of involvement in the murder of another youth named José Díaz.

As the trial wore on, Shibley asked Greenfield if she would provide summaries of each day's testimony and rulings for his review. Greenfield gladly pitched in, but as the trial wore on she became emotionally involved in the case. She was disgusted by the trial judge, Charles William Fricke, who was openly hostile to the defendants and Shibley. Greenfield also despaired about the anti-Mexican slant of the newspapers that covered the trial—especially because Fricke permitted the jurors in the trial to go home and read this negative coverage every night.

In January 1943 the jury returned guilty verdicts for all seventeen defendants. Five of them were convicted of lesser charges and released because they had already spent so much time in custody. Fricke sentenced the other twelve young men, who had been convicted of murder charges, to harsh prison sentences at San Quentin Prison. Greenfield and other supporters, though, refused to give up. Instead, they immediately formed a new group devoted to carrying on the legal fight with an appeal of the convictions.

Working for the Sleepy Lagoon Defense Committee

The acknowledged leader of this organization, which was called the Sleepy Lagoon Defense Committee (SLDC), was the respected journalist and civil rights champion Carey McWilliams. As the weeks and months passed by, though, Greenfield emerged as a central figure in the SLDC. She served as the group's executive secretary and its most tireless fundraiser, appearing before all sorts of labor unions, community organizations, and other groups to seek help with the hefty legal expenses associated with the appeals process. As the months passed by, she never lost faith in the rightness of the SLDC cause. "There are people, many people, who have a deep faith in democracy," she wrote in July 1943. "There are those who believe that democracy is the property of all the people. And that belief is not just something they sit around and talk about. It is strong enough and sincere enough to deserve action on their part. To fight a war for democracy and not fight for democracy at home would be ridiculous."[1]

Just as important as her fundraising exploits, though, was Greenfield's rapport with the so-called 38th Street Boys at San Quentin. Greenfield visited "her boys" every six weeks to keep their morale up, and she became a favored pen pal to many of them. She established enduring friendships with many of the boys and their families. Henry "Hank" Leyvas, who had been characterized by prosecutors and journalists alike as the leader of the group, became especially fond of Greenfield. Historians generally acknowledge, in fact, that he developed a severe crush on the woman.

In October 1944 all the efforts of Greenfield, McWilliams, and the rest of the SLDC paid off. The guilty verdicts were overturned by appeals court judge Clement Nye, who cited insufficient evidence and Fricke's clear bias against the defendants. The 38th Street Boys learned of Nye's decision from a joyful—and hastily written—Western Union telegram from Greenfield.

A few weeks later, Greenfield joined in the celebration when all twelve young men were formally released from prison to resume their lives. Years later, Greenfield told the *Los Angeles Times* that the appeal was the greatest event of her life.

Fighting for Social Justice

The SLDC closed its doors shortly after the Sleepy Lagoon defendants gained their release, but Greenfield kept working on social and economic justice issues for a variety of organizations. During the 1980s and 1990s, for instance, she led 85 humanitarian aid trips to war-torn Nicaragua. Greenfield even taught self-defense courses to women for several years.

Greenfield also was married three times. Her first marriage, which produced two children, ended in divorce. She then married poet Thomas McGrath in 1952. This union also ended in divorce, but she kept the McGrath surname and became known from that point forward as Alice Greenfield McGrath. Her third marriage was to martial arts instructor Bruce Tegner, who died in 1986.

When Greenfield died on November 27, 2009, many people offered testimonials to her generous spirit and passion for fighting for what she believed in. "She was one of the heroines of the 20th century," said Luis Valdez, who wrote a famous play about the Sleepy Lagoon trial called *Zoot Suit* in the 1970s. "In Los Angeles, I can't think of many people who surpass her influence."[2]

Sources:

Barajas, Frank P. "The Defense Committees of Sleepy Lagoon: A Convergent Struggle against Fascism, 1942-1944." *Aztlán: A Journal of Chicano Studies,* Spring 2006.

McGrath, Alice. "The Education of Alice McGrath." Michael Balter, interviewer. Los Angeles: Oral History Program, University of California, Los Angeles, 1987.

Pagán, Eduardo Obregón. *Murder at the Sleepy Lagoon: Zoot Suits, Race, and Riot in Wartime L.A.* Chapel Hill: University of North Carolina Press, 2003.

Notes:

[1] Barajas, Frank P. "The Defense Committees of Sleepy Lagoon: A Convergent Struggle against Fascism, 1942-1944." *Aztlán: A Journal of Chicano Studies,* Spring 2006, p. 55.

[2] Roosevelt, Margot. "Alice McGrath Dies at 92." *Los Angeles Times,* November 29, 2009. Retrieved from www.articles.latimes.com/2009/nov/29/local/la-me-alice-mcgrath29-2009nov29.

Henry "Hank" Leyvas (1923-1971)

Mexican-American Defendant in the Sleepy Lagoon Murder Trial

Enrique Henry "Hank" Reyes Leyvas was born in Tucson, Arizona, on April 24, 1923. Leyvas was the third-oldest of ten children born to his parents, Guadalupe Reyes and Seferino Gamino Leyvas. The family eventually moved to Los Angeles, where Leyvas struggled to figure out what he wanted to do with his life. Residents of his 38th Street neighborhood remembered him as a bold and charismatic young man who had a knack for fixing broken-down cars, and his younger sister Lupe described him as both smart and devoted to his family. She recalled, for example, that her older brother loved to purchase stylish zoot suits to wear at parties and dances, but that he would also set aside some of his earnings so that his mother could occasionally treat herself to silk stockings and nice perfumes. He also worked steadily after dropping out of high school, first at factory jobs and then at a modest ranch that his parents took over.

At the same time, though, Leyvas frequently clashed with the city police. He acquired numerous speeding tickets, which he apparently deserved, and in early 1942 he pled guilty to an assault charge that resulted in three months in jail and three years of probation. On multiple other occasions, though, city police arrested him on serious charges like automobile theft, armed robbery, and assault and battery. In each of these instances, Leyvas was cleared of all charges. But the experiences—which included beatings from officers while he was in custody—made him extremely distrustful of the police.

A Night of Violence

On the evening of August 1, 1942, Leyvas, his girlfriend Dora Barrios, and several other young people from the 38th Street neighborhood drove out to the Williams Ranch on the outskirts of Los Angeles for a night of making out. Leyvas and Barrios parked on the shore of Sleepy Lagoon, a popular swimming and picnicking spot. A short time later, though, Leyvas got in a verbal confrontation with a couple carloads of young men from the nearby Downey neighborhood. The clash escalated into a beating in which the Downey boys assaulted both Leyvas and his girlfriend.

After the Downey youth departed, Leyvas gathered his friends together and returned to 38th Street to make plans for a revenge attack. Leyvas had little trouble finding volunteers, especially when his friends learned that the Downey boys had used their fists on his girlfriend. A short time later, a caravan of angry young men and women from 38th Street were hurtling down country roads on their way back to the Williams Ranch.

Unable to find their attackers at Sleepy Lagoon, they headed for a birthday party that was being held by one of the families that worked at the ranch. The Downey boys were not at the party, either—they had actually been kicked out earlier in the evening—but Leyvas and his friends were so pumped up for a fight that they instigated one with the party hosts. The ugly melee lasted for about ten minutes before Leyvas and the rest of the 38th Street residents departed for home. A short time later, dazed and battered members of the birthday party found one of their guests, José Díaz, lying by the side of the road with severe injuries. He died shortly after an ambulance delivered him to a city hospital.

The Sleepy Lagoon Trial

Police investigators quickly identified Leyvas and his friends as the likely murderers. Leyvas was one of the first men arrested for the Díaz murder, and he was subjected to intense questioning from police. Leyvas, his family members, and his attorneys all claim that he was badly beaten by investigators who wanted him to confess, but Leyvas steadfastly maintained that he had nothing to do with the young man's death.

Investigators eventually put seventeen young men from the 38th Street neighborhood who had been at the Williams Ranch on trial for murder (five other accused men were eventually acquitted in separate trials). The mass trial of Leyvas and his friends was officially known as *People v. Zammora,* but the Los Angeles press dubbed it the Sleepy Lagoon murder trial. It began on October 13, 1942, and lasted for twelve weeks. During that time, the prosecution repeatedly described Leyvas as the leader of a 38th Street "gang" devoted to criminal activities. The press picked up on this description and passed it along to their readers, even though there was little evidence to support this charge. The "gang member" accusation, however, fit in neatly with the newspapers' well-established racist practice of identifying all Mexican-American "zoot suiters" as immoral juvenile delinquents.

An even bigger problem for Leyvas and his fellow defendants was the judge who oversaw their trial. Judge Charles William Fricke made little effort to disguise his dislike for the 38th Street Boys or their lawyers. In addition, he issued numerous rulings that put the defense at an extreme disadvantage. During the first month of the proceedings, for instance, he would not allow the defendants to shower, cut their hair, or change their clothes. As they became progressively shaggier and dirtier, the jurors directed increasingly scornful looks their way. Fricke also forced Leyvas and the other defendants to sit separately from their attorneys and only allowed them to speak with their attorneys when court was not in session. These rulings depriving the Leyvas and the others of their constitutional "right to counsel"—a defendant's right to unhindered consultation with his or her legal representative.

On January 12, 1943, the jury returned with guilty verdicts for all seventeen defendants, including first-degree murder convictions for the "ringleader" Leyvas and two other defendants, José Ruíz and Bobby Telles. Fricke then pronounced sentences for the 38th Street Boys. He announced life sentences for Leyvas, Ruíz, and Telles. Nine others who had been found guilty of second-degree murder were sentenced to five-years-to-life. These twelve men were promptly shipped off to San Quentin Prison to begin serving their time. The remaining five defendants were found guilty of assault, but they were released because of the amount of time they had already spent in jail.

As soon as the sentences were announced, a group of concerned citizens known as the Sleepy Lagoon Defense Committee (SLDC) launched a campaign to appeal the convictions. The SLDC received valuable assistance in their efforts from Lupe Leyvas and several other family members of the defendants. As the appeals process slowly moved forward, Leyvas and the other eleven 38th Street Boys waited helplessly in San Quentin. During this time Leyvas forged a deep friendship with Alice Greenfield, who was the SLDC's executive secretary and one of its chief fundraisers. She became an emotional anchor for Leyvas, who was extremely bitter about the trial and the general anti-Hispanic environment that had pervaded California throughout his youth. The June 1943 Zoot Suit Riots in Los Angeles further deepened his anger. At times during his stay in San Quentin this bitterness overflowed into fights with fellow inmates. At one point Leyvas was even transferred for a three-month stay at Folsom Prison, which had a higher security level than San Quentin.

In October 1944 a California court of appeals overturned all the Sleepy Lagoon convictions and dismissed all charges against Leyvas and the rest of the defendants. Leyvas was ecstatic about his release and joined in the joyful celebrations that followed. But when Leyvas returned to Los Angeles, he brought his anger and resentment with him. Within a few years of his release he was back in prison, this time for selling drugs. This news saddened and frustrated people like Greenfield and SLDC chairman Carey McWilliams, who had worked so hard to free Leyvas.

Leyvas later established a restaurant in East Los Angeles, but he never married. On July 6, 1971, he died of a heart attack in the restaurant at age forty-eight. Ben Margolis, the attorney who led the successful appeal of the Sleepy Lagoon convictions, later said that Leyvas's life was one of unfulfilled potential. "The same person, under different circumstances, would have moved toward leadership.... Of all of [the defendants], he had the greatest sense that he was a member of a group that was being walked on, being discriminated against, and that he was going to fight against it ... regardless of what would happen to him, he was totally courageous and [showed] no physical fear as far as you could tell."[1]

Sources:

Escobar, Edward. *Race, Police, and the Making of a Political Identity: Mexican Americans and the Los Angeles Police Department, 1900-1945.* Berkeley: University of California Press, 1999.

Pagán, Eduardo Obregón. *Murder at the Sleepy Lagoon: Zoot Suits, Race, and Riot in Wartime L.A.* Chapel Hill: University of North Carolina Press, 2003.

"People & Events: Enrique "Henry" Reyes Leyvas (1923-1971)." In *The American Experience: Zoot Suit Riots,* 2002. Retrieved from www.pbs.org/wgbh/amex/zoot/eng_peopleevents/p_leyvas.html.

Notes:

[1] Quoted in Pagán, Eduardo Obregón. *Murder at the Sleepy Lagoon: Zoot Suits, Race, and Riot in Wartime L.A.* Chapel Hill: University of North Carolina Press, 2003, p. 84.

Carey McWilliams (1905-1980)

American Journalist and Attorney Who Headed the Sleepy Lagoon Defense Committee

Carey McWilliams was born on December 13, 1905, in Steamboat Springs, Colorado. His father was a prominent rancher and state legislator, but his business fortunes plummeted and he committed suicide when Carey was in his mid-teens. In 1922 McWilliams moved to California, enrolling at the University of Southern California (USC). He graduated with a law degree from USC in 1927 and promptly accepted a position with a Los Angeles firm.

Left-Wing Activist and Writer

During the 1930s McWilliams became one of the best-known—and most controversial—public figures in southern California. He was deeply moved by the terrible toll that the Great Depression took on all working Americans, but the plight of Mexican migrant farm workers became a particular focus of his attention. As the 1930s unfolded McWilliams repeatedly represented farm workers who were being exploited by big white-owned agricultural operations. He also emerged as one of the state's leading progressive voices in print. McWilliams's first book had been a 1928 biography of writer Ambrose Bierce, but in the 1930s he became a fearless left-wing commentator on California culture and politics. He was a regular contributor to progressive publications like *The Nation* and *Pacific Weekly*, and in 1939 he published the best-selling *Factories in the Field.*

This investigative work charged that the state's powerful business interests had joined together to establish and maintain ruthless employment policies toward Mexican migrant families. In the words of scholar Frank Bajaras, *Factories in the Fields* documented "how the agricultural industry, working hand in hand with law enforcement agencies, had used the intimidation of workers and manipulation of the press to trample on constitutional civil liberties."[1]

In 1939 McWilliams also accepted an appointment from Governor Culbert Olson to head the state's Division of Immigration and Housing. In this capacity McWilliams pushed heavily for new laws that would boost the wages, living conditions, and working conditions of agricultural workers, but with only limited success. Nonetheless, big California growers attacked him at every turn, referring to him as "Agricultural Pest No. 1, worse than pear blight or boll weevils."[2] McWilliams was also an outspoken critic of the internment of Japanese Americans during World War II. He resigned his post in 1942, after incoming governor Earl Warren stated that his first act as governor in early 1943 would be to fire McWilliams.

McWilliams and the Sleepy Lagoon Trial

In the fall of 1942 McWilliams became deeply involved in one of the most sensational trials in the history of Los Angeles. The trial concerned seventeen Mexican-American teens and young men who had been charged in the murder of another Mexican-American youth on August 1, 1942. McWilliams lent his writing and fundraising talents to several organizations that believed that the defendants were being unfairly treated in the courts and the city's newspapers.

The so-called Sleepy Lagoon murder had become a media sensation by January 1943, when all seventeen defendants were found guilty of varying levels of involvement in the killing. The verdicts and stiff sentences did not surprise McWilliams, but they did infuriate him. As chairman of the Sleepy Lagoon Defense Committee (SLDC), he played a pivotal role in publicizing the case and gathering financial contributions so that the guilty verdicts could be appealed. In October 1944 a California appeals court overturned the guilty verdicts of all seventeen Sleepy Lagoon defendants. The court ruled that their constitutional rights had been repeatedly violated during the course of the initial trial. This legal victory has been cited by many historians as an event that spurred Hispanic Americans to become more insistent about securing their full civil rights in the 1950s and 1960s.

Challenging McCarthyism

In addition to his work with the SLDC, McWilliams was in the thick of several other high-profile issues and events of the 1940s and 1950s. He covered the 1943 Zoot Suit Riots in Los Angeles for several publications, and when the violence finally died down he called for a federal investigation of the Los Angeles Police Department. McWilliams also urged Governor Warren to establish a commission to investigate the riots. Warren did just that, and the commission's subsequent report heavily criticized the city's press and law enforcement community for their attitudes and actions toward Mexican-American citizens before and during the riots.

In the late 1940s McWilliams authored a number of important and influential books that attacked racial discrimination and bigotry in America in general and California in particular. These works included *Ill Fares the Land: Migrants and Migratory Labor in the United States* (1942), *Prejudice: Japanese-Americans, Symbol of Racial Intolerance* (1944), *Southern California: An Island on the Land* (1946), *A Mask for Privilege: Anti-Semitism in America* (1948), and *North from Mexico: The Spanish-Speaking People of the U.S.* (1949).

Another McWilliams book, published in 1950, was *Witch Hunt: The Revival of Heresy.* He wrote this work in response to the McCarthy era, a post-World War II period when millions of Americans fell victim to fears that their country was in danger of being overwhelmed by communism. The era was named for Republican senator Joseph McCarthy, who was the ringleader of feverish anti-Communist "witch hunts" in American workplaces, classrooms, and households. Throughout the late 1940s and early 1950s McWilliams regularly defended Americans who were accused by government investigators of being Communists or Communist sympathizers. McWilliams and other foes of "McCarthyism" argued that by criminalizing unpopular political philosophies and hounding people for "suspicious" friendships, American lawmakers were cowards who failed to protect their fellow Americans against an unscrupulous monster. "[McCarthy] does not need to prove a charge," McWilliams wrote. "All he needs to do is whisper 'communism' and even men sworn to uphold and protect the Constitution will act like so many sheep."[3]

At the height of McCarthyism in the early 1950s, McWilliams was repeatedly and falsely accused of being a Communist himself. But McWilliams never let these charges intimidate him. Instead, he steadily fought back against McCarthy and his many allies at every turn. As biographer Kevin Richardson wrote, "he lost several friends and associates to suicide during the McCarthy period, but even as the wages of dissent rose, he displayed cool resolve and unshakeable moral courage."[4]

At the Helm of *The Nation*

McWilliams frequently waged battle against McCarthyism and other social problems through the pages of *The Nation,* one of the country's best-known left-wing magazines. He began working for the magazine in 1951, and four years later he became its editor, a position he held for the next twenty years. During his years at the helm of the magazine he helped nurture the careers of several young journalists who would become famous during the 1960s and 1970s, including Ralph Nader and Hunter S. Thompson.

McWilliams died on June 27, 1980. His death did not attract the level of notice that one might expect of someone who had made significant contributions as a writer, journalist, social activist, and attorney. In subsequent years, however, he has been "discovered" by a growing number of civil rights activists, historians, and journalists. Historian Kevin Starr, for instance, has described McWilliams as "the single finest nonfiction writer on California—ever," while scholar Patricia Nelson Limerick called him one of "the truly ethical leaders of the American West."[5]

Sources:

Barajas, Frank P. "The Defense Committees of Sleepy Lagoon: A Convergent Struggle against Fascism, 1942-1944." *Aztlán: A Journal of Chicano Studies,* Spring 2006.

Richardson, Peter. *American Prophet: The Life and Work of Carey McWilliams.* Ann Arbor: University of Michigan Press, 2005.

Starr, Kevin. *Embattled Dreams: California in War and Peace, 1940-1950.* New York: Oxford University Press, 2002.

Notes:

1 Barajas, Frank P. "The Defense Committees of Sleepy Lagoon: A Convergent Struggle against Fascism, 1942-1944." *Aztlán: A Journal of Chicano Studies,* Spring 2006, p. 48.

2 Richardson, Peter. *American Prophet: The Life and Work of Carey McWilliams.* Ann Arbor: University of Michigan Press, 2005, p. ix.

3 Quoted in Richardson, p. 206.

4 Richardson, p. x.

5 Quoted in Richardson, p. 290.

Edward Roybal (1916-2005)
First Hispanic-American Member of the Los Angeles City Council and Longtime U.S. Representative

Edward Roybal was born on February 10, 1916, in Albuquerque, New Mexico. His family moved to the Boyle Heights barrio of Los Angeles when he was a youngster, so he ended up attending the city's Roosevelt High School. After graduating from high school in 1934 he briefly joined the Civilian Conservation Corps, then studied business and law at the University of California at Los Angeles (UCLA) and Southwestern University, respectively.

Around 1940 Roybal decided to shift his career focus to the public health field. In 1940 he became a director of health education for the California Tuberculosis Association. This position eventually evolved into the directorship of health education for the Los Angeles County Tuberculosis and Health Association, where he remained until 1949. The only interruption to this public service was a stint in the U.S. Army during World War II.

A Historic Victory

In 1947 Roybal made an unsuccessful bid for a seat on the Los Angeles City Council, a legislative body that shares responsibility with the mayor for managing the city's affairs. After the election, he concluded that he would have won had his district's Hispanic community provided greater support to him. Urged on by white and Mexican-American business leaders who had been impressed by his public health work, Roybal decided to run for election again in 1949.

The central pillar of Roybal's campaign was an organization he founded called the Community Service Organization (CSO). The CSO became a leading advocate in Los Angeles for ending discriminatory policies in the city's businesses, schools, and neighborhoods. In addition, it organized effective voter-registration drives in minority communities throughout East Los Angeles.

These new Hispanic voters lifted Roybal to victory in the 1949 city council race. He thus became the first Hispanic American to ever serve on the Los Angeles City Council. Roybal remained a councilman for the next thirteen years, during which time he became widely recognized for his efforts to increase the political and economic power of the city's Mexican-American community. Many of these efforts were undertaken in collaboration with the CSO, which fought against discriminatory practices in housing, education, and many other realms of city life. "We were able to effectuate changes that today are taken for granted by many individuals," Roybal said. "I am sure that there are many who live in [East Los Angeles] today that never knew such a struggle ever went on."[1]

On to Washington

On November 6, 1962, Roybal, a Democrat, was elected to the U.S. House of Representatives. This victory made him the first Hispanic from California to serve in the U.S. Congress since 1880. Roybal served in Congress for the next three decades as representative of a district that included East Los Angeles and parts of Hollywood and the city's downtown area.

Roybal easily won re-election fifteen times, and he became known as a staunch supporter of military veterans, bilingual education, and civil rights for minorities, elderly, and disabled Americans. He also regularly devoted time and energy to political issues of particular importance to Hispanics, such as hiring discrimination. He was also a founding member of the Congressional Hispanic Caucus, which was established in 1976.

In 1993 Roybal decided to retire from Congress, but his daughter Lucille Roybal-Allard succeeded him in the House of Representatives (she became the representative for the state's recently reshaped 33rd district, which included part of her father's old district). Roybal remained in California after his retirement, and he and his wife Lucille established a foundation dedicated to providing college scholarships to deserving students.

Roybal died on October 24, 2005, from respiratory failure, leaving behind his wife and three children. Since his passing, several educational, community, and health-related public buildings in California have been renamed in his honor, including the Edward R. Roybal Federal Building and the Edward R. Roybal Learning Center, both in Los Angeles.

Sources:

Burt, Kenneth. "Latino Los Angeles: The Promise of Politics." In Schiesl, Martin, and Mark M. Dodge, eds. *City of Promise: Race and Historical Change in Los Angeles.* Claremont, CA: Regina Books, 2006.

"Hispanic Americans in Congress, 1822-1995: Edward R. Roybal." Library of Congress. Retrieved from www.loc.gov/rr/hispanic/congress/roybal.html.

Roybal, Edward. Interview with Oscar J. Martinez, "Interview no. 184." Institute of Oral History, University of Texas at El Paso, October 23, 1975.

Notes:

[1] Roybal, Edward. Interview with Oscar J. Martinez, "Interview no. 184." Institute of Oral History, University of Texas at El Paso, October 23, 1975, p. 14.

George Shibley (1910-1989)

Defense Attorney in the Sleepy Lagoon Murder Trial

George Shibley was born on May 6, 1910, in New York City to Lebanese parents who immigrated to America in search of a better life. He spent most of his childhood, however, on the other side of the country, in Long Beach, California. He attended Stanford University and Stanford Law School, from which he earned a law degree in 1934. Shibley promptly passed the California bar exam, and by 1935 he had opened his own law offices in Long Beach.

From the outset of his legal career, Shibley was attracted to "underdogs"—people who he believed were being unfairly treated by America's legal and political systems. He represented labor unions at a time when they were frequently attacked for alleged Communist sympathies, and he often represented poor people who were accused of murder or other serious crimes. His basic reasoning, he once told the *Los Angeles Times*, was that "I felt they were entitled to a fair trial, and I thought I could get it for them."[1]

The Sleepy Lagoon Trial

Shibley's penchant for defending the poor and politically vulnerable became evident to all of California in 1943, when he joined the legal team defending seventeen Mexican-American teenagers and young men from charges that they had murdered another Hispanic youth, José Díaz, on the outskirts of Los Angeles. Police investigators charged that the defendants had capped a night of brawling and mayhem in the vicinity of a reservoir called Sleepy Lagoon by ambushing Díaz and leaving him for dead. Many white Angelenos had no doubt that the investigators' theory was true, in part because city newspapers from that period were full of sensational and deceptive stories about the menace that zoot-suited "Pachucos"—Mexican gang members, essentially—posed to the upstanding citizens of Los Angeles.

Shibley, though, believed that the prosecution's case was not very strong. In addition, he was outraged by some of the rulings made by Judge Charles

William Fricke once the trial got underway in October 1942. For example, Fricke refused to allow the defendants to change their clothes or cut their hair, and he did not allow them to speak with their lawyers when court was in session. Shibley shared the view of supporters of the defendants—known collectively as the 38th Street Boys—that these rulings predisposed the jury against the defendants and deprived the defendants of their constitutional "right to counsel"—the right to consult with the attorneys representing them in a timely fashion.

Shibley joined the trial a week after it began. Although he officially was only representing six of the defendants, as the proceedings continued, many of his objections to Fricke's management of the trial benefited all seventeen of the 38th Street Boys. Shibley recognized that if the defendants were found guilty as he anticipated, the objections he was filing during the trial would become the foundation for future attempts to appeal the verdicts and have them overturned.

Shibley's frequent objections infuriated Fricke, who treated the attorney with growing disdain as the days passed. Nonetheless, Shibley refused to back down. He raised concerns about the fairness of the trial up to the very end of the proceedings. In January 1943 the all-white jury returned with guilty verdicts for all seventeen defendants, and Fricke sentenced most of them to long prison sentences.

Shibley's objections, though, provided a legal lifeline for the Sleepy Lagoon Defense Committee (SLDC), a group dedicated to overturning the convictions. Shibley had intended to file an appeal of the convictions himself, but shortly after the trial concluded he was drafted into the military. The SLDC promptly hired Ben Margolis, who used Shibley's legal maneuvers as the basis for an appeal of the convictions. In October 1944, almost two years after the guilty verdicts had been handed down in the Sleepy Lagoon case, all of the convictions were overturned by a California appeals court. A few days later the 38th Street Boys were released and their records cleared. "Depending on how you look at it, the case made me famous or infamous," Shibley later said. "It also made the forces of law and order hate me."[2] The trial was also noteworthy for Shibley personally. He met actress Eleanor Shaw during the proceedings and married her less than a week later.

Controversial Later Career

Shibley remained a legal maverick for decades to come. Practicing with his sons William and Jonathan, he displayed a continued willingness to represent unpopular clients who he felt were not receiving their full constitutional protections. The most notorious of these later clients was Sirhan Sirhan, who had assassinated Democratic presidential candidate Robert F. Kennedy in Los Angeles in 1968. Sirhan was convicted and sentenced to death, but his mother approached Shibley in hopes that he could get the sentence reduced to one of life in prison. Shibley agreed to take the case, even though he had been an active Kennedy supporter at the time of the murder.

Shibley and two other lawyers subsequently filed an appeal on Sirhan's behalf to the California Supreme Court. Their appeal asserted that the state gave juries too much flexibility to impose the death penalty. Before their appeal was taken under consideration, though, the Court ruled in another case that California's state constitution prohibited the death penalty as cruel and unusual punishment. Sirhan's life was thus spared, though he spent the rest of his life in prison.

Shibley died on July 4, 1989, when he went into cardiac arrest while recovering from heart surgery. Attendees at his funeral included many of the former 38th Street Boys he had defended in the 1942-1943 Sleepy Lagoon trial.

Sources:

Corrales, Sue. "George Shibley Has Given Many an Underdog His Day in Court." *Los Angeles Times*, January 16, 1986. Retrieved from www.articles.latimes.com/1986-01-16/news/hl-28850_1_george-shibley.

Pagán, Eduardo Obregón. *Murder at the Sleepy Lagoon: Zoot Suits, Race, and Riot in Wartime L.A.* Chapel Hill: University of North Carolina Press, 2003.

"People & Events: George E. Shibley (1910-1989)." In *The American Experience: Zoot Suit Riots*, 2002. Retrieved from www.pbs.org/wgbh/amex/zoot/eng_peopleevents/p_shibley.html.

Notes:

[1] Quoted in Corrales, Sue. "George Shibley Has Given Many an Underdog His Day in Court." *Los Angeles Times*, January 16, 1986. Retrieved from www.articles.latimes.com/1986-01-16/news/hl-28850_1_george-shibley.

[2] Quoted in Corrales.

PRIMARY SOURCES

Anglo Squatters Swarm Mexican-Owned Haciendas in California

When the United States wrenched California out of Mexico's hands in 1848, the Californios (Catholics of Spanish descent who made their homes in California) hoped that they would be able to maintain ownership of their big ranches in the territory. Their lands, though, were openly coveted by Anglos—especially after the Gold Rush of 1849. Before long, state and federal authorities developed a wide assortment of laws and legal judgments to take Mexican-owned lands away from their longtime owners and put them in the hands of whites. The main method for accomplishing this was to force Mexican owners of land in California to negotiate a long, complicated, and expensive series of legal maneuvers to defend their property rights. In the meantime, the Californios were legally restrained from halting the flood of Anglo squatters onto their lands.

White settlers, ranchers, and miners in California had little sympathy for the Mexican hacienda owners who found themselves under siege. A few whites, however, felt that the manner in which the Californios were losing their land to the Anglo invasion amounted to little more than theft. One such Anglo was John S. Hittell. As editor and journalist for a wide range of California-based publications in the mid-nineteenth century, Hittell regularly praised California's beauty and value to the United States. In the following commentary from an 1858 issue of Hutchings' California Magazine, *though, Hittell condemns America's attitude and policies toward the Californios and their lands.*

When the great immigration of 49 filled the land [of California] with Americans, it became necessary to provide for the recognition and protection of the good Mexican [land] titles by the American Courts. But how was this to be done? By the ordinary State Courts? The judges would not be sufficiently able, and would be ignorant of the [Mexican] laws under which the grants had been made; and the juries would be composed of Americans whose interests would lead them to do injustice to the large land-owners. Besides, the lawmakers and judges elected by a deeply interested populace could not be depended upon to do justice under such circumstances.

Or should the protection be rendered by the appointment of a commission, instructed to make a summary examination of all claims, declare all those valid which had been in possession previous to the conquest, and of which some record might be found in the archives; leaving the other claims to be tried in the U.S. Courts? This was the policy which should have been pursued.

But that plan was not to prevail. Mr. [William] Gwin's bill "to ascertain and settle the private land claims in the State of California," became a law, on the 30th of March, 1851. This act provides for the appointment of a special Judicial Committee, (to be composed of three judges) before which all claimants to land, in the State, under Mexican titles, should bring suit against the Federal Government, within two years after the date of the act, under penalty of forfeiting their land....

This act provided that the owners of land should sue the Government or lose their land. But why be subjected to so severe a condition? The land owners had committed no offence, that they should be threatened with spoliation [plundering or theft]. It was not their fault that the Mexican land system differed from the American. The introduction of a new system by the Government did not justify the invalidation of titles, which had been good before, and the subjection of the owners to tedious and expensive litigation. When the American Government took California, it was in honor bound to leave the titles to property as secure as they were at the time of the transfer, and express provision to this effect was made in the treaty [of Guadalupe Hidalgo]. Let us imagine that California were to be again transferred to some other power, whose land system is far more complex and strict than our own, and that all our present titles should be declared incomplete and insecure, and that every land owner should be taxed to one-fourth of the value of his land to pay for defending his title before a foreign and hostile Court, and, if successful, should not get his title until six or eight years after the commencement of the litigation;—would we not exclaim against it as extremely unjust? But what is the difference between that supposed case and the actual one under consideration? There is no difference between the two principles involved in the two cases; each supposes a great wrong—such a wrong as has been committed by the Federal Government of the United States upon holders of land in California under Mexican grants....

It was severe hardship for owners of land under grants from Mexico, that they should be required to sue the government of the United States, (which ought to have protected—not persecuted them), or lose their land; but this hardship was rendered much more severe by the peculiar circumstances under which the suits had to be tried. The trials were to be had in San Francisco at a time when the expenses of traveling and of living in San Francisco were very great, and the fees of lawyers enormous. The prosecution of the suits required a study of the laws of Mexico, in regard to the disposition of the public lands, and this study had, of course, to be paid for by the clients. In many cases the claimants had to come to San Francisco from remote parts of the State; having three hundred miles to travel, bringing their witnesses with them at their own expense. The witnesses were nearly all native Californians, and it was necessary to employ interpreters at high prices.

Meanwhile the claimant could not dispose of his land, on account of the cloud there was on his title.... Many squatters were, no doubt, glad of a pretext under which they might take other people's land and use without paying rent.... The number of settlers or squatters [on lands owned by Mexicans in California] became large; they formed a decided majority of the voters in several of the counties; their political influence was great; politicians bowed down before them; all political parties courted them; and most of the U.S. Land Agents, and District Attorneys, appointed under the influence of the California Congressmen, became the representatives of the settler interest....

The consequence of the system was, that a large portion of the most valuable farming land in the State was occupied by squatters. This occupation contributed greatly to injure the value of the property. The land owner could not sell his land, nor use it, and yet he was compelled to pay taxes. His ranch brought serious evils upon him. It was the seat of a multitude of squatters, who ... were his bitter enemies. Cases we know, where they fenced in his best land; laid their claims between [the owner's] house and his garden; threatened to shoot him if he should trespass on their inclosure; killed his cattle if they broke through the sham fences; cut down his valuable shade and fruit trees, and sold them for fire-wood; made no permanent improvements, and acted generally as tho' they were determined to make all the immediate profit possible, out of the ranch. Such things were not rare: they are familiar to every person who knows the general course of events during the last five years in Sonoma, Napa, Solano, Contra Costa, Santa Clara, Santa Cruz and Monterey Counties....

Source:

Hittell, John S. "Mexican Land-Claims in California." *Hutchings' California Magazine,* April 1858, pp. 442-48. Retrieved from http://www.yosemite.ca.us/library/hutchings_california_magazine/22.pdf.

Examples of Anti-Mexican Discrimination in 1930s America

During the 1930s and early 1940s discrimination against Mexicans was commonplace across America. Racist attitudes were particularly strong in places like Texas and California, where Mexican immigrants were concentrated. The American public and news media paid little attention to this situation until the Zoot Suit Riots exploded in Los Angeles in mid-1943. Afterwards, American newspapers and magazines scrambled to publish stories about the riots—and the possible root causes of the violence. One such piece (excerpted here) was published by George I. Sanchez, a professor of Latin American Education at the University of Texas, in the magazine Common Ground.

Widespread attention has been drawn to the Los Angeles, California, gangs of zoot-suited, socially maladjusted, "Mexican" youngsters known as "pachucos." Mixed with the intelligent efforts and genuine concern of some public officials and laymen over the disgraceful situation which has been allowed to develop in the Los Angeles area, there is also much sanctimonious "locking of barn doors after the horses have been stolen" sort of expression and action by those whose past lack of interest and whose official negligence bred the juvenile delinquency which now plagues that city's officialdom, hinders the program of the armed forces, and embarrasses the United States before Latin America and the world.

The seed for the pachucos was sown a decade or more ago by unintelligent educational measures, by discriminatory social and economic practices, by provincial smugness and self-assigned "racial" superiority. Today we reap the whirlwind in youth whose greatest crime was to be born into an environment which, through various kinds and degrees of social ostracism and prejudicial economic subjugation, made them a caste apart, fair prey to the cancer of gangsterism. The crimes of these youths should be appropriately punished, yes. But what of the society which is an accessory before and after the fact? …

When the pachuco "crime wave" broke last year, I communicated with the Office of War Information: "I understand that a grand jury is looking into the 'Mexican' problem in Los Angeles and that there seems to be considerable misunderstanding as to the causes of the gang activities of Mexican youth in that area. I hear also that much ado is being made about 'Aztec forebears,' 'blood lust,' and similar claptrap in interpreting the behavior of these citizens.…"

The pseudo-science of the Los Angeles official who is quoted as reporting to the Grand Jury on the Sleepy Lagoon murder case that "Mexican" youths are motivated to crime by certain biological or "racial" characteristics would be laughable if it were not so tragic, so dangerous, and, worse still, so typical of biased attitudes and misguided thinking which are reflected in the practices not only of California communities but also elsewhere in this country.

The genesis of [pachuco culture] is an open book to those who care to look into the situations facing Spanish-speaking people in many parts of the Southwest. Arizona, Colorado, Texas, and, to a much lesser degree, even New Mexico have conditions analogous to those which have nurtured the California riots. In some communities in each of these states, "Mexican" is a term of opprobrium applied to anyone with a Spanish name—citizen and alien alike, of mestizo blood or of "pure white" Spanish colonial antecedents. In many places these people are denied service in restaurants, barber shops, and stores. Public parks and swimming pools, some of which were built by federal funds, are often closed to them. Some churches, court houses, and public hospitals have been known to segregate them from "whites." Separate, and usually shockingly inferior, segregated "Mexican" schools have been set up for their children. Discriminatory employment practices and wage scales, even in war industries (the President's Executive Order 8802 and his Committee on Fair Employment Practice to the contrary notwithstanding), are still used to "keep the 'Mexican' in his place."...

A Texas friend says that the Mexicans in her town had been ordered out of the parks and that Mexicans were mistreated there. Another report tells of a group of school children of Mexican and Latin American origin who went to a neighboring town "to spend the day and to attend a celebration. They decided to go swimming in a public swimming pool and they were denied entrance thereto because they were of Latin American and Mexican origin, although they permitted two Japanese children ... to enter said swimming pool." The Chancellor of a Mexican Consulate "was expelled with his wife and children from the —— swimming pool in the town of ——, Texas; the only reason given for the expulsion was that they were Mexicans." In another town "the teacher took the Latin American school children to a park ... she was told by the keeper of the park to get out as this park was not for the use of the Mexicans."

In the course of a hike, a Scoutmaster and his troop of Boy Scouts, all in uniform, were ordered out of a public park where they had stopped to rest, because they were "Mexicans." A group of American citizens of Mexican descent, on the verge of joining the Army, "were denied entrance to the swimming pools because they were 'Latin Americans'." Soldiers in the uniform of the

United States Army have been refused service in public places because they were "Mexicans," several of them having been ejected when they insisted on buying a cup of coffee, a hamburger, or a bottle of beer....

A pathetic letter from a descendant of the colonial settlers of Texas states: "Do you think there is any hope of getting our problems solved? We wish you would do something to help us. We are being mistreated here every time we turn around. We are not allowed in cafes, movies, restaurants. Even Latin Americans in United States Army uniforms are sometimes told they can't see a show because the Mexican side is full. In the public schools our children are segregated. They are given only half a day's school because of the teacher shortage, while the others have full-time classes. There is no teacher shortage for them. Please tell us if there is anything to do about it. We wrote a letter to the Office of Civilian Defense, Washington, D.C. But we haven't heard from them. We don't know if that is the right place to write to or not." ...

In another town, on the Fourth of July, "several hundred citizens of the United States of Mexican extraction were told over the loud speaker that they should go home because the dance being held in a public square was for white people only. Among the persons ejected were many wearing United States soldier's uniforms." At still another place, again on the Fourth of July, at an American Legion dance, Spanish-name veterans of World War I were asked to leave because the dance was for "whites" only....

Many communities provide a separate school for children of Spanish name. These "Mexican schools" are established ostensibly for "pedagogical [educational] reasons," thinly veiled excuses which do not conform with either the science of education or the facts in the case. Judging from current practice, these pseudo-pedagogical reasons call for short school terms, ramshackle school buildings, poorly paid and untrained teachers, and all varieties of prejudicial discrimination. The "language handicap" reason, so glibly advanced as the chief pedagogical excuse for the segregation of these school children, is extended to apply to all Spanish-name youngsters regardless of the fact that some of them know more English and more about other school subjects than the children from whom they are segregated. In addition, some of these Spanish-name children know no Spanish whatsoever, coming from homes where only English has been spoken for two generations or more.

The community mores suggested in the above illustrations do not reflect simply the attitudes of untutored masses. Equally glaring, un-American practices are carried on by those of privileged social and economic status. The basic real estate contracts in many subdivisions in several Texas cities provide that "neither they, nor their heirs, executors, administrators, or assigns, shall sell or lease any portion of said property to any person of Negro blood, or Mexicans." Another far too common provision in deeds stipulates that: "No lot or part of lot in said addition at any time may be occupied by or used by any person except those of the Caucasian race. This provision shall be so construed as excluding from occupancy in said subdivision Mexicans, Latin Americans, Negroes, and people of the yellow race." Wealthy, highly educated, prominent Latin Americans, some citizens of the United States and some citizens of prestige of Mexico and of other Latin American countries, have been refused the right to purchase or occupy property in those subdivisions....

On July 12, 1941, before the pachuco question had become a matter of general interest, a Spanish American from California summarized the situation this way: "The so-called 'Mexican Problem' is not in fact a Mexican problem. It is a problem foisted by American mercenary interests upon the American people. It is an American problem made in the U.S.A." He was protesting the movement then on foot to permit the indiscriminate and wholesale importation of laborers from Mexico. In response to such protests steps were taken by the governments of the United States and of Mexico to protect both the imported alien and the residents of this area from the evils inherent in such letting down of the bars, evils of which ample evidence was furnished during World War I under similar circumstances. Today, however, the pressure of vested interests is finding loopholes in that enlightened policy and, again, the bars are rapidly being let down.

Si Casady of McAllen, Texas, in an editorial in the *Valley Evening Monitor* hits the nail on the head when he says: "There is a type of individual who does not understand and appreciate the very real dangers inherent in racial discrimination. This type of individual does not understand that his own right to enjoy life, his own liberty, the very existence of this nation and all the other free nations of the world depend utterly and completely on the fundamental principle that no man, because of race, has any right to put his foot upon the neck of any other man.... "

The Spanish-speaking people of the United States need to be incorporated into, and made fully participating members of, the American way of life. The "Mexican" needs education, he needs vocational training and placement in American industry on an American basis, he needs active encouragement to participate in civic affairs and to discharge his civic obligations, and he needs constant protection by public officials from the pitfalls into which his cultural differences may lead him or into which he may be forced by unthinking sectors of the public.

The record, briefly reported here, of oppressive self-righteousness and the "incidents" to which it has led is an appalling one. Even more frightening are the prospects of a future when such cheaply hatched social attitudes and practices come home to roost as the full-fledged and expensive spectres of crime, disease, ignorance, internal discord, and international enmity. One generation's sins of "racial" oppression on the part of a majority sector of the population are indeed visited upon its progeny, many fold. The fruits of "racial" discrimination are boomerangs—seeds which breed, in the majority group, fascism and tolerance of the concentration camp for "inferior races." The vicious practices referred to above do harm to the "Mexican," yes. However, infinitely more harm is done to the group which perpetrates or tolerates the practices. The pachuco is a symbol not of the guilt of an oppressed "Mexican" minority but of a cancerous growth within the majority group which is gnawing at the vitals of democracy and the American way of life. The pachuco and his feminine counterpart, the "cholita," are spawn of a neglectful society—not the products of a humble minority people who are defenceless before their enforced humiliation.

Source:

Sanchez, George I. "Pachucos in the Making." *Common Ground,* Autumn 1943, pp. 13-20.

Depression-Era Los Angeles Targets Mexicans for Repatriation

The March 1933 issue of the American Mercury, *one of the leading U.S. magazines of the era, featured a hard-hitting commentary on California's Depression-era efforts to "repatriate" Mexican immigrants—push them back over the border into Mexico. The article was penned by liberal lawyer and journalist Carey McWilliams, who became a fierce and well-known advocate for politically powerless people of all races during the 1930s and 1940s. In his* American Mercury *piece, McWilliams uses sarcasm and satire to emphasize his belief that white Angelenos glossed over Mexican unhappiness with repatriation policies. At various points in his commentary, for instance, McWilliams delivers a mocking echo of the rationalizations that white Californians embraced to excuse their behavior. In the final paragraph, though, McWilliams drops his mask and closes his commentary with the story of a sorrow-filled young Mexican girl whose life has been turned upside-down by repatriation.*

In 1930 a fact-finding committee reported to the Governor of California that, as a result of the passage of the Immigration Acts of 1921 and 1924, Mexicans were being used on a large scale in the Southwest to replace the supply of cheap labor that had been formerly recruited in Southeastern Europe. The report revealed a concentration of this new immigration in Texas, Arizona, and California, with an ever increasing number of Mexicans giving California as the State of their "intended future permanent residence." It was also discovered that, within the State, this new population was concentrated in ten southern counties.

For a long time Mexicans had regarded Southern California, more particularly Los Angeles, with favor, and during the decade from 1919 to 1929 the facts justified this view. At that time there was a scarcity of cheap labor in the region, and Mexicans were made welcome. When cautious observers pointed out some of the consequences that might reasonably be expected to follow from a rash encouragement of this immigration, they were shouted down by the wise men of the Chamber of Commerce. Mexican labor was eulogized as cheap, plentiful, and docile. Even so late as 1930 little effort had been made to unionize it....

During this period, academic circles in Southern California exuded a wondrous solicitude for the Mexican immigrant. Teachers of sociology, social service workers, and other subsidized sympathizers were deeply concerned about his welfare. Was he capable of assimilating American idealism? What anti-social traits did he possess? Wasn't he made morose by his native diet? What could be done to make him relish spinach and Brussels sprouts? What was the percentage of this and that disease, or this and that crime, in the Mexican population of Los Angeles? How many Mexican mothers fed their youngsters according to the diet schedules promulgated by the manufacturers of American infant foods? In short, the do-gooders subjected the Mexican population to a relentless barrage of surveys, investigations, and clinical conferences.

But a marked change has occurred since 1930. When it became apparent last year that the programme for the relief of the unemployed would assume huge proportions in the Mexican quarter, the community swung to a determination to oust the Mexicans. Thanks to the rapacity of his overlords, he had not been able to accumulate any savings. He was in default in his rent. He was a burden to the taxpayer. At this juncture, an ingenious social worker suggested the desirability of a wholesale deportation. But when the Federal authorities were consulted they could promise but slight assistance, since many of the younger Mexicans in Southern California were American citizens, being the American-born children of immigrants. Moreover, the Federal officials insisted, in cases of illegal entry, upon a public hearing and a formal order of deportation. This procedure involved delay and expense, and, moreover, it could not be used to advantage in ousting any large number.

A better scheme was soon devised. Social workers reported that many of the Mexicans who were receiving charity had signified their "willingness" to return to Mexico. Negotiations were at once opened with the social-minded officials of the Southern Pacific Railroad. It was discovered that, in wholesale lots, the Mexicans could be shipped to Mexico City for $14.70 per capita. This sum represented less than the cost of a week's board and lodging. And so, about February, 1931, the first trainload was dispatched, and shipments at the rate of about one a month have continued ever since. A shipment, consisting of three special trains, left Los Angeles on December 8. The loading commenced at about six o'clock in the morning and continued for hours. More than twenty-five such special trains had left the Southern Pacific station before last April.

No one seems to know precisely how many Mexicans have been "repatriated" in this manner to date. The *Los Angeles Times* of November 18 gave an estimate of 11,000 for the year 1932. The monthly shipments of late have ranged from 1,300 to 6,000. The *Times* reported last April that altogether more than 200,000 repatriados had left the United States in the twelve months preceding, of which it estimated that from 50,000 to 75,000 were from California, and over 35,000 from Los Angeles county. Of those from Los Angeles county, a large number were charity deportations....

One wonders what has happened to all the Americanization programmes of yesteryear. The Chamber of Commerce has been forced to issue a statement assuring the Mexican authorities that the community is in no sense unfriendly to Mexican labor and that repatriation is a policy designed solely for the relief of the destitute even, presumably, in cases where invalids are removed from the County Hospital in Los Angeles and carted across the line. But those who once agitated for Mexican exclusion are no longer regarded as the puppets of union labor.

What of the Mexican himself? The repatriation programme apparently, is a matter of indifference to this amiable ex-American. He never objected to exploitation while he was welcome, and now he acquiesces in repatriation. He doubtless enjoys the free train ride home. Probably he has had his fill of bootleg liquor and of the mirage created by pay-checks that never seemed to buy as much as they should. Considering the anti-social character commonly attributed to him by the sociological myth-makers, he has cooperated nicely with the authorities. Thousands have departed of their own volition. In battered Fords, carrying two and three families and all their worldly possessions, they are drifting back to *el terenaso*—the big land. They have been shunted back and forth across the border for so many years by war, revolution, and the law of supply and demand, that it would seem that neither expatriation or repatriation held any more terror for them.

The Los Angeles industrialists confidently predict that the Mexican can be lured back, "whenever we need him." But I am not so sure of this. He may be placed on a quota system in the meantime, or possibly he will no longer look north to Los Angeles as the goal of his dreams. At present he is probably delighted to abandon an empty paradise. But it is difficult for his children. A friend of mine, who was recently in Mazatlan, found a young Mexican girl on one of the southbound trains crying because she had to leave Belmont High School. Such an abrupt severance of the Americanization programme is a contingency that the professors of sociology did not anticipate.

Source:

McWilliams, Carey. "Getting Rid of the Mexican." *American Mercury,* March 1933, pp. 322-324.

A Los Angeles Police Officer Issues a Racist Report on the Mexican "Element"

After Los Angeles County convened a grand jury for the Sleepy Lagoon case, jury members heard testimony from several law enforcement officials who stated that Mexican-American youth were more genetically inclined to commit crimes than their white counterparts. This racist theory was made most forcefully by Lieutenant Edward Duran Ayres, chief of the Foreign Relations Department of the Los Angeles County Sheriff's Department. In both a formal report and grand jury testimony, Ayres urged that authorities implement "drastic measures" to counteract Mexican Americans' "biological" tendency to engage in "gangsterism." Following are excerpts from Ayres's notorious submission to the Sleepy Lagoon grand jury.

There are a number of factors contributing to the great proportion of crime by a certain element of the Mexican population. Among the contributing factors are those of economics, lack of employment, and small wages that cause certain ones to commit theft and robbery for the purpose of obtaining the means to own and drive automobiles and to have money to spend on their girl friends, liquor, clothes, etc., also to obtain the wherewithal to live.

Mexicans as a whole in this country are restricted in the main to only certain kinds of labor and that being the lowest paid. It must be admitted that they are discriminated against and have heretofore practically been barred from learning trades, etc....

Economic conditions in their home life is of course not conducive to a higher standard of living and consequently a lower perspective of responsibility and citizenship is the result. Lack of recreation centers is another factor.

Discrimination and segregations as evidenced by public signs and rules such as appear in certain restaurants, public swimming plunges, public parks, theatres and even in schools, causes resentment among the Mexican people.... Broken homes, liquor, loose morals, are also contributing factors. All of these, and other factors, are the cause of the Mexican youth remaining within their own racial groups, resulting in what is now practically gang warfare—not only among themselves but also between themselves and the Anglo-Saxons.

But to get a true perspective of this condition we must look for a basic cause that is even more fundamental than the factors already mentioned, no matter how basically they may appear. Let us view it from the biological basis—in fact, as the main basis to work from. Although a wild cat and a domestic cat are of the same family they have certain biological characteristics so different that while one may be domesticated the other would have to be caged to be kept in captivity, and there is practically as much difference between the races of man as so aptly recognized by Rudyard Kipling when he said when writing of the Oriental, "East is East and West is West, and never the twain shall meet," which gives us an insight into the present problem because the Indian, from Alaska to Patagonia, is evidently Oriental in background—at least he shows many of the Oriental characteristics, especially so in his utter disregard for the value of life.

When the Spaniards conquered Mexico they found an organized society composed of many tribes of Indians ruled by the Aztecs who were given over to human sacrifice. Historians record that as many as 30,000 Indians were sacrificed on their heathen altars in one day, their bodies being opened by stone knives and their hearts torn out while still beating. This total disregard for human life has always been universal throughout the Americas among the Indian population, which of course is well known to everyone....

Mexico has a population of approximately 20,000,000 people, of which less than 20% are pure Caucasians or White. The remaining population are Indian and Mestizos, or a mixture of the Caucasian and Indian....

The revolution that started in Mexico under Madera in 1910 had as its objective the freeing and betterment of the Indian, and also much of the Mextizo element, from peonage. Many social experiments were tried out ... but all ended in apparent failure. Mexican authorities state that in spite of every well meant social reform and leniency shown to a certain element under the program of rehabilitation the said element has not responded to their hopes, and that even from the economic standpoint, when higher wages are given and an opportunity for a higher standard of life is opened to them, instead of availing themselves of that opportunity they prefer to work half a week instead of a whole week, and we find that same condition here in a great many instances among this same element....

The Mexican Indian is mostly Indian—and that is the element which migrated to the United States in such large numbers, and looks upon leniency by authorities as an evidence of weakness or fear, or else he considers that he was able to outsmart the authorities. Whenever this element is shown leniency in our courts, or by our probation officers and other authorities ... he becomes a hero among his own gang members and boasts that the law was afraid to do anything to him or else that the authorities were dumb and that he put it over on them. However, whenever this Mexican element receives swift and sure punishment such as proper incarceration, he then, and then only, respects authorities. It is just as essential to incarcerate every member of a particular gang, whether there be 10 or 50, as it is to incarcerate one or two of the ring leaders....

Many of these young gangsters have comparatively good jobs, so economics is not a determining factor in their case. In fact, as mentioned above, economics as well as some of the other features are contributing factors, but basically it is biological—one cannot change the spots of a leopard.

The Caucasian, especially the Anglo-Saxon, when engaged in fighting, particularly among youths, resort to fisticuffs and may at times kick each other, which is considered unsportive, but this Mexican element considers all that to be a sign of weakness, and all he knows and feels is a desire to use a knife or some lethal weapon. In other words, his desire is to kill, or at least let blood....

There is a feeling among the Mexican population that they have not even the control over their children that they would have in Mexico, because if they try to restrain their children and punish them for going out nights, a complaint is made against them and they are [hauled] into court for punishing their children. Therefore, the youth is allowed to run wild—both boys and girls. There is also a notable lack of cooperation on the part of the parents with the authorities....

A law enforcement officer can only work with the tools he is furnished with—he does not make the laws. If drastic measures are not taken to put an end to gangsterism it will increase, with resultant murders, and that which none of us want to see—race riots—especially at a time like this when we need the friendship and cooperation of Latin America [in fighting Germany and Japan]....

Again, let us repeat—the hoodlum element as a whole must be indicted as a whole. The time to rehabilitate them is both before and after the crime has been committed, as well as during his incarceration, but it appears useless to turn him loose without having served a sentence. As stated above, he considers it an act of fear or weakness on the part of the authorities.... We also recognize the fact that the great majority of the Mexican people here are law abiding, and are just as anxious as we are to prevent crime among this element, as they rightly consider that it is a reflection on the Mexican population as a whole. They state they are most anxious to cooperate with the authorities to end this intolerable condition. They state it is a shame and a crime that a certain small percentage of the entire Mexican population should jeopardize the friendly relations and good will that so long have prevailed. They consider, and rightly so, that they are an integral part of American society.

Source:

Ayres, Edward Duran. "Statistics: The Nature of the Mexican American Criminal," 1942. Reprinted as Appendix A in Jones, Solomon James. *The Government Riots of Los Angeles, June 1943: A Thesis.* Los Angeles: University of California, Los Angeles, 1969, pp. 85-88.

Courtroom Clashes between Fricke and Shibley

The Sleepy Lagoon Trial included numerous instances of tense verbal sparring between Los Angeles County Superior Court judge Charles William Fricke and lead defense attorney George Shibley. During the trial proceedings, Shibley repeatedly registered his unhappiness with decisions by Fricke that clearly helped the prosecution. Angered and embarrassed by Shibley's objections, Fricke ridiculed and insulted the defense attorney with growing frequency as the trial wore on.

One of their testiest clashes came on the afternoon of Thursday, November 12, 1943. After dismissing the jury for the day, Fricke rebuked the defense team for disobeying previous instructions not to meet with their clients during recesses. As the following excerpt from the court transcript shows, Fricke's criticism sparked an angry response from Shibley, who accused the judge of blatantly violating the civil rights of the Sleepy Lagoon defendants.

THE COURT: Just a minute, gentlemen. I want counsel to sit down here a minute. I am just getting thoroughly tired of this situation. I am going to ask counsel to just listen for a moment while the court reads something. I referred on October 21st to the difficulty we were having, by a confusion that was caused — I made this statement: "There is another thing I want stopped very definitely, and that is when we take a recess I want these defendants — there are a large number of them — taken to the prisoners' room and I do not want anybody to stop those prisoners and try to talk to them. If counsel want to talk to their clients they will have to do it at some other time."

Now, I said that and I meant it. I am not going to tolerate any violation of the orders of this court. Counsel who disobey that injunction are guilty of contempt of court. I am not going to proceed in that matter, but if it happens again I am going to take very severe action. I want to call attention to the fact this is the third time I have had to mention it, and it is going to be the last.

While I am talking I want to call counsel's attention to something else, and that is to huddles in the hallway between counsel and witnesses and counsel and members of the families, and also to conversations on the elevators. To my own knowledge that has also been violated, and if that order is violated something is going to happen....

MR. SHIBLEY: If your Honor please, I was not here in the case when that first order that your Honor read was made. However, at this time, if your Honor please, I do wish to take exception to it and also make the demand at this time that my defendants, all of them, be allowed to sit with me at the counsel table.

And I am going to cite to your Honor the case of *Commonwealth v. Boyd,* 246 Pennsylvania, page 529, which I believe is followed in this jurisdiction.

THE COURT: That request will be denied. Furthermore, your excuse does not go very far, because the second time I had occasion to mention it, I called your attention to page 213 and requested that you read it. That was directed to you personally. Now, if you did not follow the court's request, I am not responsible for it.

MR. SHIBLEY: If your Honor please, I still make the request, and I do wish to make a showing in the record here, that it is relatively impossible for me to conduct my defense of my defendants without being able to consult with them and sit with them, and talk with them during the presentation of the prosecution's case. I am also going to say this for the record: That the defendants in the position in which they are seated are seated in a column of seats in very much the fashion as prisoners in a prisoners' box, and the jury are looking at them all the time sitting in that prisoners' box. And I say, for the record, that seated as they are, the purpose of it or, at least, the effect of it is to prejudice these defendants in the minds of the jury. And I am going to cite your Honor's action in having them seated there and in refusing them the right to consult with counsel during the trial and talk with their attorneys during the trial in the courtroom, as misconduct, and ask the jury be admonished to disregard the fact that they are seated in the place that they are, and ask your Honor to point out to the jury the fact they are seated there does not impute that they are guilty or that there is any suspicion that they are guilty of a crime.

(Applause by some spectators.)

THE COURT: Mr. Bailiff, I want you to take every — wait a minute, every one of those persons that applauded, I want you to place them under arrest and bring them before the court for contempt of court....

MR. SHIBLEY: Before we leave this subject, I also want the record to show that during the entire trial that several witnesses for the People have been seated either at or near the counsel table and the attorneys for the People have consulted with them, have talked to them during the course of the trial. And I also wish it to show —

THE COURT: May I suggest the difficulty you are in is the difficulty that always attends counsel who comes in after the trial is started. Now, that matter was taken care of and it was covered by the record. If there is any question as to witnesses who were in the courtroom who ought not to be here, that matter can be taken care of.

MR. SHIBLEY: I am not raising that objection, and I believe your Honor understands I am not.

THE COURT: That is what I thought you were driving at.

MR. SHIBLEY: I am simply contrasting the treatment of the witnesses for the People and the treatment of the defendants with respect to their right to consult with their counsel and sit with them. Now, as it happens, if your Honor please, the only time I or other counsel can be apprised as to whether or not it is necessary for us to go up and see our defendants in the attorneys' room upstairs, is if these defendants want either at the conclusion of the trial or at the recess to speak to us and say, "There is something I want to tell you about that." And that is the reason I went over here because a couple of these boys were telling me that they wanted to see me about something that came up during the day's trial. If I am to be denied that right, then I cannot properly represent my defendants.

THE COURT: That can be taken care of without causing that disturbance which we had every time the prisoners were taken out of the courtroom. We have got twenty-two prisoners here, and ordinarily one or two bailiffs to handle the situation; that is all we can possibly get. The minute one defendant is stopped and held up by counsel it means that the entire group is held up and stopped. …

MR. SHIBLEY: Will your Honor state for the record now what I am alleged to have done that created a disturbance with reference to talking to these two defendants?

THE COURT: You went over and were leaning over a group of the defendants, and Mr. Schutz was doing the same thing at the time the court was still in session; the jury was not in session as a jury, but were going out and we had taken the recess for a purpose that had absolutely nothing to do with the taking of testimony.… There are certain things counsel cannot do in the courtroom, and I am not going to permit them. We have to conduct these trials in an orderly manner, and we cannot reach over. As far as the witnesses you have referred to, those are officers and it was agreed those officers might stay here and might remain here at the counsel table with the District Attorney. That was agreed upon by counsel before you got into the case and now you are objecting to it.

MR. SHIBLEY: I am not objecting to that, but I do think, if your Honor please, that I have the same right and my defendants have the same right to consult with one another intimately during the course of the conduct of this trial.

THE COURT: I am not objecting to that at all.

MR. SHIBLEY: I make that demand, and I ask that some arrangement be made by which the defendants may sit with their counsel during the trial.

THE COURT: It is impossible to make that arrangement. It is perfectly obvious when one man represents a number of defendants he cannot sit next to each one of them, nor is it possible around the counsel table to consult with twenty-two defendants. It just cannot be done. If you want to consult with your clients during the course of the trial, that is perfectly all right. You have done it and Miss Zacsek has done it, and other attorneys have done it. I am not objecting to that. What I am objecting to is the disorderly manner in which it is done. That will be all....

MR. SHIBLEY: If your Honor please, I know your Honor said something in your remarks about no restriction being placed upon these defendants except that they had to be in the courtroom. May I inquire of your Honor if, under that view that your Honor has given, it is proper for the defendant Victor Thompson to rise from his seat where he is seated,— and what I refer to in my motion as the prisoners' dock,— and to walk over to the counsel table and consult with me during the trial?

THE COURT: I certainly won't permit it.

MR. SHIBLEY: You will not permit it?

THE COURT: No.

MR. SHIBLEY: Well, that is just the sort of thing I am making an objection to.

THE COURT: All right, then. I understand thoroughly.

MR. SHIBLEY: If your Honor please, I object on the grounds that that is a denial of the rights guaranteed all defendants, and each one of them, both by the Federal and State constitutions. I think their right to consult and to be represented by counsel at all stages of the proceedings demands that they have the right to come to their counsel during the proceedings and speak to them.

THE COURT: Well, that is your opinion. I happen to have another one.

MR. SHIBLEY: And I do so demand that they be given those rights.

THE COURT: I am not going to tolerate defendants walking around the courtroom of their own sweet desire.

MR. SHIBLEY: I do not ask for that.

THE COURT: The opportunity to consult exists, but not the opportunity to walk around the courtroom every time that one of them felt that they would like to walk to the counsel table....

MR. SHIBLEY: I do insist also, if your Honor please, that some reasonable arrangement be made so that these defendants will be able to consult with their counsel throughout the entire proceeding. If your Honor takes exception to counsel going over to the box and speaking to these defendants at recesses, your Honor, I ask that your Honor keep the court in session for a reasonable time so that counsel can step over and talk to the defendants at each recess and determine whether or not it is necessary for the attorneys to go upstairs to the attorneys' room to consult with them further.

THE COURT: The court is not going to keep these prisoners in here at recesses in the courtroom, the entire group of persons, because one counsel wants to talk to one defendant. I think I have covered that pretty thoroughly.

MR. SHIBLEY: Then, if your Honor please, I take it at any recess no counsel is permitted to approach any of the defendants or say anything to him; is that correct?

THE COURT: Without first securing permission of the court, yes....

Source:

The People of the State of California, Plaintiff and Respondent vs. Gus Zammora [sic], et al., Defendants and Appellants: Reporter's Transcript on Appeal. Volume 6. November 12, 1942, pp. 2798-2816. Department of Special Collections, University of California at Los Angeles Library.

Trying to Survive the Zoot Suit Riots

Beatrice Griffith was a social worker who worked with Mexican-American families in Los Angeles in the early 1940s. After the Zoot Suit Riots took place, Griffith wrote a short story, "In the Flow of Time," that dramatized the event. The author drew on her own experiences during the riots, as well as newspaper accounts of the mob violence. Griffith's story centers around two Mexican-American friends from Los Angeles who are scheduled to be inducted into the army during World War II. On their last weekend before induction they go visit the narrator's grandfather on his farm outside the city. They spend the day hunting rabbits, talking about their girlfriends, and speculating about life in the army. Before returning to the city they change into zoot suits because they want to look good for a party later that night. When they return to Los Angeles, though, they find their city in a state of violent upheaval. Following is a brief excerpt from Griffith's story, which was published in 1948 in a magazine called Common Ground *and in a collection of Griffith's short fiction called* American Me.

It was like the sailors and marines were taking over the whole city.... They had bottles and belts, clubs and iron pipes in their hands. They were waving them over their heads. We got pushed against the building by the crowd who was looking up the street where there was a lot of shouting and where somebody was getting beaten. The people were filling the streets, packing them from building to building, yelling like they were drunk or crazy. They didn't see us yet 'cause we had on leather coats and they couldn't see our pants in the mob. The air was full of excitement....

Then we heard a roar and somebody yelled, "They got 'em, they got 'em. They got those goddamned zootsuiters." And from the corner in front of the theater a mob of sailors poured out with a couple of kids wearing fingertip coats, pulled along in the middle of them. Those kids were getting it all right, with busted heads and bleeding faces—those kids were getting it. Pretty soon, a black coat was thrown up and got passed around with people catching it and tossing it. Then the pants came and another coat, a tan one. Each time the crowd yelled and packed tighter to the center. The police were standing along the sides holding their night sticks, looking pleased about the whole thing. Or maybe they were gazing at the stars in the sky. They didn't do nothing to stop that mob....

We ran down the alley until we got to the next street. The mob was bigger here, there were thousands of 'em everywhere. Traffic had stopped and the sirens were screaming. Even the ambulances had a hard time pushing through....

Source:

Griffith, Beatrice. "In the Flow of Time." *Common Ground,* September 1948, pp. 13-20.

Mexican-American Activists Assess the Causes of the Zoot Suit Riots

In the wake of the Zoot Suit Riots, a number of Los Angeles-based civil rights organizations issued statements and reports about the disturbance and its root causes. One such group was the Los Angeles Committee for American Unity, which was chaired by Vince Monroe Towsen Jr. Other members of the committee included Carey McWilliams, Clore Warne, Al Waxman, Charlotta A. Bass, Eduardo Quevedo, Ben Margolis, and Manuel J. Avila.

The following is an excerpt from a June 11, 1943, memorandum on the Zoot Suit Riots written by the committee. The memo was sent to California attorney general Robert W. Kenny and Bishop Joseph T. McGucken, who had been appointed by Governor Earl Warren to chair a special investigative committee on the rioting and its causes. Many of the points made here by the Los Angeles Committee for American Unity eventually made it into McGucken's influential final report.

Although it appears from a reading of the newspapers that the current disturbances were caused by a tremendous crime wave participated in by so-called "zoot suit" gangsters, the riots cannot be explained upon that basis. In the first place, the number and severity of crimes committed by the "zoot-suiters" has been gravely exaggerated and proof that all of the crimes charged against these groups were committed by them is utterly lacking. The available facts indicate that while there has been some increase in crime among the Mexican-American youth, some of whom wear "zoot suits," this has not been any greater than has been the increase in crimes among juveniles generally. However, by featuring all crimes committed by groups or individuals of Mexican extraction, and by exaggerating these crimes both as to number and severity, the press has created the false impression now existing in the minds of the public generally that any individual who wears a zoot-suit is a criminal and a gangster.

This false public impression has been aided by wholesale arrests of the youths wearing this type of clothing and Mexican-American youth generally, whether or not the individuals arrested were even suspected of having committed any crime. The discriminatory treatment both in the press and by the police is now extended beyond Mexican-American youth to other minority groups, particularly Negroes.

The fact that discrimination was and is directed against the two racial minorities mentioned rather than against devotees of a certain type of clothing is demonstrated by the fact that Filipino youth and others who affect this type of clothing have not been molested. Many Mexican-American and Negro youth, who did not wear and who have never worn clothing of this type were amongst those treated with the greatest severity.

For instance, one John Zion, Negro churchman and defense worker was beaten so severely that his mouth required stitching, and one Louis W. Jackson, Negro defense worker in the L.A. Shipyards, father of three young children, was attacked by some 75 soldiers, one of whom stabbed out Jackson's right eye. At the time the latter incident occurred, Jackson was returning to his home after purchasing two magazines from a newsstand just a few blocks from his home. Neither of these men wore "zoot suits" nor have they any criminal record and both were defense workers....

We have evidence of a very clear and convincing character that the police not only stood by and permitted the rioting without interference, but that they actually assisted the rioters by clearing the streets of women and very young children in anticipation of the activities of the rioters, and then disappearing and leaving the rioters a clear road for their criminal activities. In other instances they actually encouraged the sailors and soldiers to proceed with their assaults and rioting, and in still other instances actually participated in the brutal beatings which occurred. In the cases where they stood by, they frequently placed under arrest the victims of the assaults while permitting and encouraging the perpetrators thereof to go off and continue similar assaults in other parts of the city. Similarly, the Military and Naval police made no effective effort to restrain the activities of the men in the armed service.

Reliable affidavits establish that on Tuesday, June 8th, 1943, soldiers used army jeeps to transport themselves from one scene of rioting to another. Also that on another occasion naval cars were used to block off a street in the Mexican-American community while naval personnel, who had ridden to the scene in those cars, and others systematically beat up and otherwise manhandled all of the Mexican-American youths that they could find in the vicinity, at the same time causing great damage to private business enterprises and property in the area.

The rioting was not confined to the streets. Street cars were stopped; and the motormen were forced to open the doors and the rioters went through the cars and removed persons of Mexican-American nationality and Negroes and proceeded to assault them viciously. Servicemen rioters forced their way into the theaters in various parts of the cities, made the theater managers turn on the house lights and conducted a systematic search among the audiences for men and boys of these minority races. Negroes and Mexican-Americans were taken from the theaters and unmercifully beaten. In several cases the men were taken from the side of their wives, children, and parents....

For a period of several weeks the Los Angeles metropolitan newspapers; Los Angeles *Examiner,* Los Angeles *Times*, Los Angeles *Daily News*, Los Angeles *Evening Herald & Express*, have been playing up arrests of boys of the Mexican and Negro minority groups. Similar minority offenses have been played up as "Zoot Suit Gang Attacks." Quite recently two stories crossed the desks of the local editors. In one case four men of the U.S. armed forces allegedly kidnapped a young woman ... whose husband is in the U.S. armed forces, took her to an auto court and criminally attacked her. At the same time a story came to the desks of the local editors in which two young Mexican-American women were allegedly attacked by several young Mexican-American boys after they had all gone out for an automobile ride. In the case of the attack by the Mexican boys, the newspapers ran large headlines in the front pages of their newspapers, "Zoot Suit Boys Attack Young Mother."

In the case of the four servicemen, who took the young wife of the soldier to the auto court, the story appeared on approximately pages 10 or 12 of the same newspapers. This same approach has been followed by local newspapers for a period of weeks until the general public has been led to believe that every Mexican-American youth is a gangster....

[Since the first day of the riots] local newspaper headlines have been written in such a way to heighten the interest of the community in order to sell newspapers. At the same time, various interested groups are being pitted against each other through the efforts of these stories. A study of the newspapers stating the cases will reveal that the servicemen are emphasized as being without fault and being heroes [and the papers are] attributing all fault to the so-called "zoot-suiters" and going so far as calling the Mexican-American youths rioters.

Although the servicemen participating in the numerous acts of violence and lawlessness are guilty of violations of law, it is not they who are the prime movers of this sequence of events. Rather it is the newspapers and the police who must bear the principal onus for these outbreaks. The riot hysteria of the servicemen was only a natural result of the campaign of propaganda and incitement against these minority groups....

Source:

Los Angeles Committee for American Unity. "Investigations of the Los Angeles Committee for American Unity, June 11, 1943 [letter]." Reprinted as Appendix D in Jones, Solomon James. *The Government Riots of Los Angeles, June 1943: A Thesis.* Los Angeles: University of California, Los Angeles, 1969, pp. 101-104.

The *Los Angeles Times* Attacks Eleanor Roosevelt's Stance on the Riots

In the days following the Zoot Suit Riots, many Americans drew a clear link between the violence that befell Los Angeles and racist attitudes held by white Angelenos. One of the most prominent critics to blame the riots on racial prejudice was Eleanor Roosevelt, wife of President Franklin D. Roosevelt. On June 17, 1943, newspapers all across the country published an Associated Press wire story that detailed the First Lady's comments.

These criticisms greatly alarmed Los Angeles officials, business leaders, and newspaper publishers. They belatedly recognized that if the violence was seen as a race riot, it might leave a lasting stain on the city's reputation. With this in mind, the publishers of the Los Angeles Times *issued an editorial condemning Roosevelt for her remarks.*

Following are two articles. The first is the original Associated Press story of June 17, 1943, that carried Roosevelt's remarks. The second is the editorial response from the Los Angeles Times, *published one day later.*

FIRST LADY TRACES ZOOT RIOTS TO DISCRIMINATION

Mrs. Franklin D. Roosevelt said today that she thought the zoot suit fights which have flared in Los Angeles could be traced to what she called long-standing discrimination against Mexicans in that part of the country.

The President's wife told her press conference that race problems are growing in the United States and all over the world and "we must begin to face [them]."

"For a long time I've worried about the attitude toward Mexicans in California and the States along the border," Mrs. Roosevelt said.

She asserted that the fights between zoot suit clad Mexican youths and servicemen in Los Angeles "have roots in things which happened long before."

Mrs. Roosevelt explained that she did not think the situation was simply a race problem or a youth problem but was provoked by "elements which had little to do with youth."

Secretary of State [Cordell] Hull told his press conference the zoot suit situation in Los Angeles is well in hand, thanks to effective co-operation among the Army, Navy, and municipal authorities there.

* * *

MRS. ROOSEVELT BLINDLY STIRS RACE DISCORD

It seems incredible that the wife of the President of the United States in wartime would deliberately seek to create a vicious international racial antagonism without a foundation in fact. Yet Mrs. Eleanor Roosevelt in her public statement Wednesday that zoot suit fights in Los Angeles are due to long-standing discrimination against Mexicans here says something that is as untrue as it is dangerous.

For one thing, it shows ignorance.

For another, it shows an amazing similarity to the Communist party line propaganda, which has been desperately devoted to making a racial issue of the juvenile gang problem here.

If Mrs. Roosevelt had troubled really to investigate, she would have discovered that everybody here in a position to assay the facts—including Mexican leaders, officials, the Army and Navy and civic investigators—knows that the zoot suit fights were not based on racial antagonism at all. When servicemen set out to avenge attacks which had been made on them by zooters, they were not looking for Mexicans, Negroes, or Anglo-Saxons—they were looking for the weird costumes worn by the gangsters, who have included many races.

The cry that Mexicans were being abused was not raised by Mexicans or persons of Mexican descent, but by pressure and political groups who always avidly seize upon any pretense to fan race discord.

As for "long-standing discrimination" against Mexicans here, Mrs. Roosevelt ignores history, fact, and happy tradition. California is a State that grew out of Spanish and Mexican civilization and it has always been rather ostentatiously proud of it. We have bragged of our Spanish and Mexican missions. We have paid homage and honor to the Californians of Mexican descent among us. Probably the most popular public official in Southern California is Sheriff Eugene Biscalluz, proud scion of a California family. The most beloved entertainment group in California's famous fiestas is the Jose Arias musical family, worthy Mexican descendants. We have the largest Mexican colony in the United States here and we enjoy fraternizing with them. We have been solicitous for their welfare in times of depression. We proudly maintain Olvera St.—a bit of Old Mexico—as a constant reminder of our affection for and our cordial relations with our sister republic.

We like Mexicans and we think they like us.

They know and we know that zoot suitism is a passing phase, a juvenile problem that we have to solve together. Nobody here but those who seek to create strife is making the wild accusations about "race riots" and "race discrimination."

Not a single Mexican citizen has been involved yet in the zoot riots, according to the American State Department; all the boys have been American born, no matter what their racial background.

Mrs. Roosevelt with characteristic lack of understanding has added nasty fuel to a propaganda fire, at a moment when all the people really interested in restoring order and getting at the basis of sound corrective measures felt they were succeeding.

Mrs. Roosevelt for reasons of her own has joined others, including Col. [Robert R.] McCormick of the *Chicago Tribune*, in twisting the zoot trouble into something that it isn't—a race-hatred problem.

She has contributed greatly toward misunderstanding with our Latin-American friends and allies.

Sources:

Associated Press, "First Lady Traces Zoot Riots to Discrimination." *Los Angeles Times*, June 17, 1943, p. A1.

"Mrs. Roosevelt Blindly Stirs Race Discord." *Los Angeles Times*, June 18, 1943, p. A4.

New Hispanic Hopes and Dreams in the Post-World War II Era

In 1949 a World War II veteran named Edward Roybal became the first Hispanic American in Los Angeles history to win election to the Los Angeles City Council. He spent the next decade serving the people of his Boyle Heights district. In 1962 he won election to the U.S. House of Representatives, where he served for the next three decades. In 1975—midway through his long and distinguished career in Congress—Roybal sat down for an interview with Latin American history scholar Oscar J. Martinez. In the following excerpt from that interview, Martinez (signified as M) and Roybal (R) discuss the legislator's early life in Los Angeles, some of his early civil rights victories in the city, and the major role that Hispanic military veterans played in the Hispanic civil rights movement of the late 1940s and 1950s.

M: Were your thoughts on what you wanted to do—to become an accountant—atypical for the goals that other Mexican American youngsters like yourself were setting for themselves at that time?

R: Oh yes, most definitely. In fact, it was most difficult for anyone who *could* get good grades to be in the "in" with the Spanish-speaking group. In order for us to be in the "in" we had to be around a "C" student. There were many times when we knew we could do a lot better and *could* become "A" students and do the work that was necessary to get those "As." We neglected it simply because of the attitude that existed not only on the part of [the] Spanish-speaking, but also on the part of the educators of the time. I just felt [at that time] that they were not really interested in having a Spanish-speaking person become an all "A" student. For example, in the field of track ... I wasn't an excellent athlete but I was the best they had. And I *still* don't remember a coach actually sitting down with me and encouraging me—telling me that I could win the game or giving me pointers as to what I could do to improve my stride. But I remember that same coach doing that with many others that I used to beat every week.

M: What did you run, Congressman?

R: My main race was the quarter mile: I ran, also, the hurdles. As you know, in the quarter mile the matter of stride, rhythm, and so forth is most important. Well, I don't remember coach ever sitting down and talking to me about my rhythm—how I could improve it—anything about my wind. I could see the dif-

Reprinted with permission. University of Texas at El Paso Library Special Collections Department. Interview with Edward Roybal by Oscar Martinez, Interview no. 184.

ference in the way *I* was treated with that of the Anglo who was beaten by me every week. That, now that I think back to it, was a form of subtle discrimination that, again, is hard for a young boy to understand.

M: Did you feel a strong need to achieve at that time?

R: Oh yes, most definitely.

M: To what source do you trace the origin of this feeling?

R: I think poverty more than anything else. I grew up, as I've said, in these areas. I come from a large family. We went through a Depression. I had to work during the time that my father was ill because he would not accept relief. It was this poverty atmosphere that we grew in, I think, that provided the drive that was necessary to achieve certain things. I did not achieve everything I wanted to and everything that I felt that I could have. On the other hand, going into the field of politics, I have made available opportunities for others. I feel that the one job that *I* have is not to do something for people, but to make it possible for people to do something for themselves. *That* is what I strive to do. I don't want anyone to do anything for me and I don't know of anyone that *wants* anybody to do anything for them—that is, anybody worth their salt. So, my philosophy is that if I can do something that will open up opportunities for individuals and give them a chance to do something for themselves, *that* is the best service that can be performed....

[Roybal then discusses how the ethnic pride in his Mexican-American community gave him strength.]

It was something then that gave strength to one's belief that there was something beyond the so-called poverty atmosphere. Even though there was a great deal of struggle that had to go on *before* we got out of it and a great deal of suffering, we still looked beyond the point which we were in, looking forward at all times to better days. This is what I mean about the matter of the discrimination. First of all, [there] existed the pride in the home and then our ultimate desire to do something about it [discrimination]. There were many instances in the Boyle Heights area [when] we were children. For an example, when Evergreen Playground was open they wouldn't permit a Mexican American student to go bathing except on a Tuesday. There was a barber shop that's still there; it was called the "Leader Barber Shop." It's on Brooklyn and Soto. [The barber shop] wouldn't cut a Mexican's hair. I, for an example, went to get my hair cut there. I saved money to do it because this was more or less a status symbol, getting your hair cut at the Leader Barber Shop. [I] was told that I had to have an appointment. When I tried to make an appointment, they wouldn't give it to me. I argued and finally they told me that they would cut my hair but they'd have to throw the comb away after they did so. Well, this was right in the Boyle Heights area. Now, coming from that particular atmosphere in which you had to go through this struggle—going back to the home and feeling this great family pride, the togetherness of the family—and then trying to look to the future was a most difficult thing, because the obstacles were too great. But, nevertheless, that drive, I think, comes about *because* of the cohesiveness of the family and *because* one helped the other in this particular struggle, and because one is so understanding about the things that I have described with regard to discrimination. They understand how one feels; one goes home and tells the family about this, and then the encouragement that comes at the dinner tables gives us all kinds of things: "This people are just ignorant people. We were here before the Pilgrims landed. We have as much right to the United States as they have and perhaps even more, and eventually through education we will be able to have them understand that this right is an equal right." All these things that go on in a family—I think they go on in *every* family in different ways. I think it was really the background that has made it possible not only for me, but for other Mexican Americans, to acquire some measure of success.

[Roybal then discusses his successful 1949 campaign to become the first Hispanic member of the Los Angeles City Council.]

My campaign committee became the Community Service Organization; I organized it.... It was a most successful venture. We had an average of 450 people coming to every meeting every week. We had committees all over, fighting [for] different causes. We registered [people to vote] and ended up with a net of over 11,000 people. Incidentally, we're talking about Spanish-speaking people now, so you can just imagine how many people we had to register in the Boyle Heights area, where the Spanish-speaking people was only 20 percent, to get 11,000. So these 11,000 people, then, were contacted and gotten to the polls, and that's how I got elected. *Because* of that organization, we fought many causes.... The CSO was also responsible for one other thing that I think is most important. Many people don't know [about it]. I went out purposely to try to buy a house at the real estate office located on the corner of Beverly Boulevard and Atlantic Avenue in East Los Angeles. I went into the office, told them that I wanted a house by a certain number because at that time all that area was being developed with new houses. I gave the man a check for $250 which, incidentally, I *didn't* have in the bank, but nevertheless took a chance. He, in an embarrassed way, told me that it wasn't his fault but he couldn't sell to a Mexican. I took my card out and gave it to him. I was already a member of the Los Angeles City Council—this was the first week that I served as a member of the City Council. I gave him my card and walked to my car. By the time I got to my car, which took maybe thirty seconds, he was right behind me and said, "I can sell to you because you're different." ...

I went back to the Los Angeles City Council and reported this incident. That got publicity, I think, in every major newspaper in the United States—that a GI had been refused GI housing in the city of Los Angeles. That, then, forced these people to sit down and negotiate with us, and they opened up the project so that Mexican Americans were sold housing. The same thing was true in Montabello and in Monterrey Park. Again, we went through the same process and were able to change things in those areas where one could not buy a home unless [the buyer] were either Spanish or Italian or Argentine. But if you said that you were of Mexican descent or looked like a Mexican, like I do for an example, [you] could *not* buy a home in those areas during that time. The CSO was responsible for that change....

M: What were some of the major obstacles that you faced from the majority community in trying to organize around these issues, in trying to get yourself elected, and what were some of the obstacles in the *Mexican* community that CSO faced?

R: Well, first of all, we'll take the obstacles in the so-called dominant community, and there were *none* because it was one of complete indifference. They thought we would never be able to do anything. They never did anything to help us and, consequently, [they] generated an atmosphere of complete indifference and let us go about our business. Within the Mexican American community the motivation, I think, came from the fact that most of those who organized CSO were World War II veterans. We knew that we were equal in the battlefield—that we had all of Europe and all of the Pacific in which to die—but we seemed not to have a place at home in which to live in peace, in which to have equality in employment and so forth. It was because of *that* particular situation that the CSO became a reality. These people [were] fighting for some of these rights that we had already fought for and actually were gained in the battlefield by some of those in our own family who gave their life in Europe and the Pacific.... Now, looking at this thing from the standpoint of the overall Spanish-speaking community and leaving out those who were *not* World War veterans, I would say that there was a very sympathetic attitude. The attitude [was], "Well, let's see if we can't do *something.*" I don't think that that same attitude prevailed during the '60s and it may not even prevail today. Fighting for issues means unity, and you can't fight for an issue if there is disunity within your ranks....

M: Congressman, what effect did World War II have on Chicanos who came back from that conflict into the communities and started working for the betterment of these communities?

R: Well, unfortunately, I have to give a lot of credit to World War II from that standpoint. Had World War II not taken place, we wouldn't have the advances that we have today. I say that because the man who went from the barrio to the Army and to the Armed Forces as a whole, found that he was equal on the battlefield—getting more Congressional Medals of Honor, for instance, than any other ethnic group in the United States.... When we came back we said, "If we were equal on the battlefield, why can we not be equal here? Why can we not buy a home? Why can we not have the same opportunities in education, the same opportunities in everything else? This is our country. We already lost our brothers." I lost two, for an example. "We've already given this." I think that this is what awakened us more to the fact that we had to fight for these things.... And I say it's *unfortunate* that it took a war to finally get us to come to that realization.

Source:

Roybal, Edward. Interview by Oscar J. Martinez. "Interview no. 184," October 23, 1975. Institute of Oral History, University of Texas El Paso. Retrieved from Institute of Oral History at http://digitalcommons.utep.edu.

From the Barrio to a German POW Camp—and Back

As many as half a million Hispanic men served in the U.S. Armed Forces during World War II. One of these men was Tony Aguilera, a young man who grew up in extreme poverty in East Los Angeles before joining the army in 1942. In a 2002 interview, Aguilera recalled growing up in a Los Angeles barrio in the 1920s and 1930s, a period when most Mexican-American families in the city (and across the country) struggled mightily to make ends meet. Like many young Hispanic men of that era, Aguilera served in the U.S. Armed Forces during World War II. His military experience brought him both great happiness and great terror. Aguilera established friendships that transcended racial barriers in the army, and he felt a sense of brotherhood with fellow World War II veterans that lasted for the rest of his life. But the war also introduced him to the terrors of the battlefield and of being captured by German troops.

Even though Tony Aguilera's childhood in an East Los Angeles barrio was once marked by poverty, he remembers it fondly.

"We were a very happy family," he said of his Mexico-born parents and 13 siblings. "We played marbles and tops and flew kites. We went to the fields and caught rabbits."

Aguilera would leave his home and fond memories behind when, on March 4, 1942, he was drafted into the service as a member of a Texas infantry unit in Europe. Eventually, he'd become a prisoner of war in a German camp for 16 months.

But during a recent interview at an East Los Angeles veterans' center, Aguilera opted to remember happier days of his youth before recounting tales of war.

As he entered his teenage years, girls, beer and popular tunes replaced marbles, tops and kites as his primary focus. In those days, he and other young people from the barrio would catch a streetcar for seven cents to Main Street, where they'd take in a show for a nickel and a nightcap of root beer at the local hangout.

"We'd play records at church, drink beer in the orchards and go to the show," reminisced Aguilera with a smile.

Reprinted courtesy of VOCES Oral History Project (formerly the U.S. Latino & Latina WWII Oral History Project), University of Texas at Austin, www.lib.utexas.edu/voces.

Life wasn't completely carefree for him, however. He took a job to support his family, and in doing that, it became necessary to acquire a certain street savvy. When food was scarce, he'd help scavenge for discarded morsels.

"My dad worked for 25 cents an hour on a farm," Aguilera said. "We found work wherever we could. The farms would throw away seconds, so we would bring them home. We survived. Someone was always hustling for something. We just wanted to make it."

It wasn't long before thoughts of just wanting to "make it" gave way to prayers of survival. Soon, Aguilera was resigned to the possibility of having to make the ultimate sacrifice for his country.

"I thought we were going to go over there and get killed, [but] I went, it was my duty. I had it in my mind I was never going to get back."

With tears welling in his eyes, Aguilera then remembers the dark days leading to his capture. With a thick layer of fog surrounding them, he and his squad, the 143rd Infantry Division 36th Infantry, entered Salerno, Italy. The squad, a Texas infantry division of mostly Latinos, was charged with getting as close to the beach as possible, dig in and hold their position.

The mission would prove treacherous and deadly.

"Only 20 some were left at the end," Aguilera recalled.

The ferocity of the battle came as something of a surprise, as the fog had camouflaged the German enemy troops. It was only after the fog dissipated that the sheer numbers of the enemy became evident.

"When we got there, there was no resistance," said Aguilera, leaning forward as he recounted the tale. "We stopped and got all our ammo out. When the fog lifted, we were surrounded. Everyone was shooting at us. You stood up and they knocked you down."

During the crossfire, Aguilera caught shrapnel in his left leg. He spent several hours in the trenches, resigned to his eventual capture by the Germans.

"I rolled over and found a nice gutter and stayed there until the Germans picked me up. They told me to get up, but I couldn't. I showed them my leg," he said. "The Germans took my pistol, grenades, ammunition and everything. They put me in a tank and took me to a hospital."

Aguilera spent three months recuperating before the Germans transferred him to Stalag 2B, a prisoner-of-war camp in Hanover, Germany. He spent 16 months as a POW before American and Russian troops liberated the camp in 1945, bringing an end to his 2 1/2-year involvement in the war.

Although he has no regrets about his wartime experience, Aguilera said he wouldn't wish the experience on anyone: "I did my share ... that's something you never forget; you don't want nobody else to go through."

After the war, Aguilera returned to East Los Angeles, where he lives today with his wife, Molly, of 60 years. But settling back into a regular life wasn't always easy. "I used to have nightmares," said Aguilera, hanging his head low. "My wife said I'd get up in the night and yell."

With time, his post-war trauma passed. But recognition for his service was harder to come by than his recovery, ironically, from members of his own ethnic group.

"The Mexicans who worked with me, they never believed me," said Aguilera, referring to his co-workers at Kal Kan Foods, where he was employed for 40 years after the war. "No one believes you. They say, 'Oh, that dumb Mexican has never been out of this country,"' he said. "Unless he's also a veteran, then he understands."

Aguilera was no stranger to ethnic slurs, even as a child. "They'd call you greaseball and stuff," he said, recalling his days in a segregated school. "You were just a dumb Mexican. I got used to it. What are you going to do, kill everyone who calls you a dumb Mexican? No, you just let it go."

Conversely, Aguilera doesn't recall any bias while in the service. It was only before and after the war, in his hometown, where he endured the insults.

As he relives his wartime experience, Aguilera feels content in his postwar life in Los Angeles, where he's surrounded by grandchildren. Along with fulfillment, he has earned a military pension. He joked about the amount he gets today versus the soldiers' pay so long ago.

"I got $10 per month. Now it's $2,000 a month! I wish I had got it when I was young," he said. "We could have gone on vacation!"

Source:

Flory, Yasemine. Interview with Tony Aguilera by Milton Carrero Galarza, March 23, 2002. VOCES Oral History Project, University of Texas at Austin.

A Landmark Legal Decision for Mexican Americans

In early 1954 the U.S. Supreme Court agreed to review the case of Hernandez v. The State of Texas. *The defendant in the case was Pete Hernandez, a Mexican-American migrant farm worker who in 1950 had been convicted of murdering a fellow migrant worker in Edina, Texas. Hernandez's attorney, a smart and experienced Hispanic-American lawyer named Gustavo Garcia, filed an appeal of the conviction. Garcia noted that the jury that convicted Hernandez was all white—and that the county in which he was convicted had systematically excluded people of Mexican origin from serving on juries for at least the past twenty-five years. Garcia charged that such exclusions, which were commonplace on juries in more than seventy counties across the state of Texas, violated the U.S. Constitution's Fourteenth Amendment, which guarantees "equal protection" to all citizens.*

The U.S. Supreme Court heard oral arguments for the case on January 11, 1954. Garcia made his arguments with assistance from lawyers from the American G.I. Forum and the League of United Latin American Citizens. On May 3, 1954, the Court announced its decision. It unanimously ruled in favor of Hernandez and ordered that his conviction be overturned. The Hernandez v. Texas *decision was a landmark legal victory for Hispanic Americans, and it constituted the first of several important civil rights victories for Hispanics during the second half of the twentieth century. Following are excerpts from the Court's decision, which was announced by Chief Justice Earl Warren.*

The systematic exclusion of persons of Mexican descent from service as jury commissioners, grand jurors, and petit jurors in the Texas county in which petitioner was indicted and tried for murder, although there were a substantial number of such persons in the county fully qualified to serve, deprived petitioner, a person of Mexican descent, of the equal protection of the laws guaranteed by the Fourteenth Amendment, and his conviction in a state court is reversed.

(a) The constitutional guarantee of equal protection of the laws is not directed solely against discrimination between whites and Negroes.

(b) When the existence of a distinct class is demonstrated, and it is shown that the laws, as written or as applied, single out that class for different treatment not based on some reasonable classification, the guarantees of the Constitution have been violated.

(c) The exclusion of otherwise eligible persons from jury service solely because of their ancestry or national origin is discrimination prohibited by the Fourteenth Amendment.

(d) The evidence in this case was sufficient to prove that, in the county in question, persons of Mexican descent constitute a separate class, distinct from "whites."

(e) A prima facie [presentation of initial evidence to support a legal claim] case of denial of the equal protection of the laws was established in this case by evidence that there were in the county a substantial number of persons of Mexican descent with the qualifications required for jury service but that none of them had served on a jury commission, grand jury or petit jury for 25 years.

(f) The testimony of five jury commissioners that they had not discriminated against persons of Mexican descent in selecting jurors, and that their only objective had been to select those whom they thought best qualified, was not enough to overcome petitioner's prima facie case of denial of the equal protection of the laws.

(g) Petitioner had the constitutional right to be indicted and tried by juries from which all members of his class were not systematically excluded.

MR. CHIEF JUSTICE WARREN delivered the opinion of the Court.

The petitioner, Pete Hernandez, was indicted for the murder of one Joe Espinosa by a grand jury in Jackson County, Texas. He was convicted and sentenced to life imprisonment. The Texas Court of Criminal Appeals affirmed the judgment of the trial court. Prior to the trial, the petitioner, by his counsel, offered timely motions to quash the indictment and the jury panel. He alleged that persons of Mexican descent were systematically excluded from service as jury commissioners, grand jurors, and petit jurors, although there were such persons qualified to serve residing in Jackson County. The petitioner asserted that exclusion of this class deprived him, as a member of the class, of the equal protection of the laws guaranteed by the Fourteenth Amendment of the Constitution. After a hearing, the trial court denied the motions. At the trial, the motions were renewed, further evidence taken, and the motions again denied. An allegation that the trial court erred in denying the motions was the sole basis of petitioner's appeal. In affirming the judgment of the trial court, the Texas Court of Criminal Appeals considered and passed upon the substantial federal question raised by the petitioner. We granted a writ of certiorari to review that decision.

In numerous decisions, this Court has held that it is a denial of the equal protection of the laws to try a defendant of a particular race or color under an indictment issued by a grand jury, or before a petit jury, from which all persons of his race or color have, solely because of that race or color, been excluded by the State, whether acting through its legislature, its courts, or its executive or administrative officers. Although the Court has had little occasion to rule on the question directly, it has been recognized since *Strauder v. West Virginia* that the exclusion of a class of persons from jury service on grounds other than race or color may also deprive a defendant who is a member of that class of the constitutional guarantee of equal protection of the laws. The State of Texas would have us hold that there are only two classes—white and Negro—within the contemplation of the Fourteenth Amendment. The decisions of this Court do not support that view. And, except where the question presented involves the exclusion of persons of Mexican descent from juries, Texas courts have taken a broader view of the scope of the equal protection clause.

Throughout our history differences in race and color have defined easily identifiable groups which have at times required the aid of the courts in securing equal treatment under the laws. But community prejudices are not static, and from time to time other differences from the community norm may define other groups which need the same protection. Whether such a group exists within a community is a question of fact. When the existence of a distinct class is demonstrated, and it is further shown that the laws, as written or as applied, single out that class for different treatment not based on some reasonable classification, the guarantees of the Constitution have been violated. The Fourteenth Amendment is not directed solely against discrimination due to a "two-class theory"—that is, based upon differences between "white" and Negro.

As the petitioner acknowledges, the Texas system of selecting grand and petit jurors by the use of jury commissions is fair on its face and capable of being utilized without discrimination. But as this Court has held, the system is susceptible to abuse and can be employed in a discriminatory manner. The exclusion of otherwise eligible persons from jury service solely because of their ancestry or national origin is discrimination prohibited by the Fourteenth Amendment. The Texas statute makes no such discrimination, but the petitioner alleges that those administering the law do.

The petitioner's initial burden in substantiating his charge of group discrimination was to prove that persons of Mexican descent constitute a separate class in Jackson County, distinct from "whites." One method by which this may be demonstrated is by showing the attitude of the community. Here the testimony of responsible officials and citizens contained the admission that residents of the community distinguished between "white" and "Mexican." The participation of persons of Mexican descent in business and community groups was shown to be slight. Until very recent times, children of Mexican descent were required to attend a segregated school for the first four grades. At least one restaurant in town prominently displayed a sign announcing "No Mexicans Served." On the courthouse grounds at the time of the hearing, there were two men's toilets, one unmarked, and the other marked "Colored Men" and "Hombres Aqui" ("Men Here"). No substantial evidence was offered to rebut the logical inference to be drawn from these facts, and it must be concluded that petitioner succeeded in his proof.

Having established the existence of a class, petitioner was then charged with the burden of proving discrimination. To do so, he relied on the pattern of proof established by *Norris v. Alabama.* In that case, proof that Negroes constituted a substantial segment of the population of the jurisdiction, that some Negroes were qualified to serve as jurors, and that none had been called for jury service over an extended period of time, was held to constitute prima facie proof of the systematic exclusion of Negroes from jury service. This holding, sometimes called the "rule of exclusion," has been applied in other cases, and it is available in supplying proof of discrimination against any delineated class.

The petitioner established that 14% of the population of Jackson County were persons with Mexican or Latin-American surnames, and that 11% of the males over 21 bore such names. The County Tax Assessor testified that 6 or 7 percent of the freeholders on the tax rolls of the County were persons of Mexican descent. The State of Texas stipulated that "for the last twenty-five years there is no record of any person with a Mexican or Latin American name having served on a jury commission, grand jury or petit jury in Jackson County." The parties also stipulated that "there are some male persons of Mexican or Latin American descent in Jackson County who, by virtue of being citizens, householders, or freeholders, and having all other legal prerequisites to jury service, are eligible to serve as members of a jury commission, grand jury and/or petit jury."

The petitioner met the burden of proof imposed in *Norris v. Alabama.* To rebut the strong prima facie case of the denial of the equal protection of the laws guaranteed by the Constitution thus established, the State offered the testimony of five jury commissioners that they had not discriminated against persons of Mexican or Latin-American descent in selecting jurors. They stated that their only objective had been to select those whom they thought were best qualified. This testimony is not enough to overcome the petitioner's case....

Circumstances or chance may well dictate that no persons in a certain class will serve on a particular jury or during some particular period. But it taxes our credulity to say that mere chance resulted in there being no members of this class among the over six thousand jurors called in the past 25 years. The result bespeaks discrimination, whether or not it was a conscious decision on the part of any individual jury commissioner. The judgment of conviction must be reversed.

To say that this decision revives the rejected contention that the Fourteenth Amendment requires proportional representation of all the component ethnic groups of the community on every jury ignores the facts. The petitioner did not seek proportional representation, nor did he claim a right to have persons of Mexican descent sit on the particular juries which he faced. His only claim is the right to be indicted and tried by juries from which all members of his class are not systematically excluded—juries selected from among all qualified persons regardless of national origin or descent. To this much, he is entitled by the Constitution.

Reversed.

Source:

Hernandez v. Texas, 347 U.S. 475 (1954).

Honoring the Heritage and Contributions of Hispanic Americans

Over the past half-century, Americans of Hispanic descent have found much greater levels of acceptance in mainstream American society. During that time, in fact, the U.S. government's efforts to celebrate Hispanic-American culture and recognize Hispanic-American contributions to the nation have greatly expanded. In 1968, for example, President Lyndon B. Johnson established Hispanic Heritage Week to formally recognize the contributions of American citizens whose ancestors came from Spain, Mexico, Central and South America, and the Caribbean. This observation was expanded by President Ronald Reagan in 1988 into National Hispanic Heritage Month, a period that runs from September 15 to October 15 every year. This thirty-day period was selected because the anniversaries of independence for many Latin American nations fall within it.

Every year since then, the U.S. Congress has formally recognized the arrival of National Hispanic Heritage Month. Following is the text of the 2011 resolution that was introduced into the U.S. Senate by Senator Robert Menendez (D-NJ), who is himself of Hispanic descent. The resolution, which details the many ways in which Hispanic Americans have become an essential part of the fabric of American life, was passed by unanimous consent.

Whereas beginning on September 15, 2011, through October 15, 2011, the United States celebrates Hispanic Heritage Month;

Whereas the Census Bureau estimates the Hispanic population in the United States at almost 50,500,000 people, making Hispanic Americans the largest ethnic minority within the United States;

Whereas 1 in 5 United States public school students is Hispanic, and the total number of Hispanic students enrolled in public schools in the United States is expected to reach 28,000,000 by 2050;

Whereas the purchasing power of Hispanic Americans is nearly $1,000,000,000,000, and there are more than 2,300,000 Hispanic-owned firms in the United States, supporting millions of employees nationwide and greatly contributing to the economic sector, especially retail trade, wholesale trade, food services, and construction;

Whereas Hispanic Americans serve in all branches of the Armed Forces and have bravely fought in every war in the history of the United States;

Whereas, as of May 31, 2011, there are 29,204 Hispanics serving with distinction in Afghanistan and Iraq;

Whereas 140,000 Hispanic soldiers served in the Korean War;

Whereas more than 80,000 Hispanics served in the Vietnam War, representing 5.5 percent of individuals who made the ultimate sacrifice for their country in that conflict even though Hispanics comprised only 4.5 percent of the United States population at the time;

Whereas, as of May 31, 2011, 605 United States military fatalities in Iraq and Afghanistan have been Hispanic;

Whereas, as of September 30, 2009, there were approximately 1,332,033 Hispanic veterans of the United States Armed Forces;

Whereas 41 Hispanic Americans have received the Congressional Medal of Honor, the highest award for valor in action against an enemy force that can be bestowed upon an individual serving in the United States Armed Forces;

Whereas Hispanic Americans are dedicated public servants, holding posts at the highest levels of government, including 1 seat on the Supreme Court, 2 seats in the Senate, 24 seats in the House of Representatives, and 2 seats in the Cabinet; and

Whereas Hispanic Americans harbor a deep commitment to family and community, an enduring work ethic, and a perseverance to succeed and contribute to society: Now, therefore, be it

Resolved, That the Senate—

(1) recognizes the celebration of Hispanic Heritage Month from September 15, 2011, through October 15, 2011;

(2) esteems the integral role of Latinos and the manifold heritage of Latinos in the economy, culture, and identity of the United States; and

(3) urges the people of the United States to observe Hispanic Heritage Month with appropriate programs and activities that appreciate the cultural contributions of Latinos to American life.

Source:

Recognizing Hispanic Heritage Month and Celebrating the Heritage and Culture of Latinos in the United States and the Immense Contributions of Latinos to the United States, S. Res. 267, 112th Cong., 1st sess. (September 14, 2011). Retrieved from http://thomas.loc.gov/cgi-bin/query/z?c112:S.RES.267.

IMPORTANT PEOPLE, PLACES, AND TERMS

Amerindians
Native peoples of North, Central, and South America.

Angelenos
Residents of Los Angeles, California.

Anglos
White Americans.

appeal
A request for a legal review of a case that has already been decided by a court of law, in hopes of having the verdict overturned.

assimilate
To integrate or blend into a wider culture or other type of group.

barrio
Mexican-American neighborhood.

Bowron, Fletcher (1887-1968)
Mayor of Los Angeles during the Sleepy Lagoon trial and Zoot Suit Riots.

Bracero Program
A U.S. federal program enacted with the cooperation of the Mexican government that sought to attract Mexican workers to American farms; first begun in 1942 to relieve war-related labor shortages, it was maintained until 1964.

caste system
A social structure that organizes and divides people on the basis of their inherited ethnic and economic status.

Chicano
A term for Mexican Americans that first became heavily used in the 1960s and 1970s.

Communist
Someone who believes in communism, a political philosophy that eliminates private property and places all goods and property in the hands of government authorities who distribute those resources equally.

defendant
A person accused of a crime or other legal violation in a court of law.

demographics
The characteristics of a population, such as age, income, education level, and ethnic background.

Díaz, José (1919-1942)
The Mexican farm worker whose murder resulted in the Sleepy Lagoon trial.

fascism
A radical political philosophy that places higher value on nationality or race than on the individual; governments based on fascism are often dictatorships that see violence and intimidation as legitimate tools for suppressing or stamping out opposition.

Fricke, Charles William (1882-1958)
Judge who presided over the 1943 Sleepy Lagoon murder trial.

grand jury
A type of jury composed of citizens that decides whether to bring formal criminal charges—an indictment—against someone accused of committing a criminal act.

Greenfield, Alice (1917-2009)
Canadian-American civil rights activist and member of the Sleepy Lagoon Defense Committee.

Hispanic
A person in the United States of Spanish-speaking origin or ancestry.

indictment
Formal accusation that someone has committed a crime.

juvenile delinquent
A person under the age of eighteen who participates in criminal activity.

Latin America
Region of the world encompassing South America, Central America, and the various islands of the Caribbean.

Latino American
An American whose family has ancestral ties to Latin America.

Leyvas, Henry "Hank" (1923-1971)
The most highly publicized Mexican-American defendant in the Sleepy Lagoon murder trial.

McWilliams, Carey (1905-1980)
American journalist and attorney who headed the Sleepy Lagoon Defense Committee.

mestizo
A person with one Indian and one Spanish parent.

mulatto
A person with one African and one Spanish parent.

pachuca
A female version of the pachuco.

pachuco
A male Mexican-American youth or young man who favors zoot suits and adopts a rebellious lifestyle; among older Hispanics the term also is sometimes used to refer to troublemakers and criminals.

repatriados
Mexicans and Mexican Americans who either voluntarily left or were forced to leave the United States in the 1930s.

Roybal, Edward (1916-2005)
First Hispanic-American member of the Los Angeles City Council and longtime U.S. representative.

Ruíz, Manuel, Jr. (1905-1986)
Hispanic-American activist in Los Angeles who helped found the Coordinating Council for Latin American Youth (CCLAY).

segregation
Separation of people by race or ethnicity.

Shibley, George (1910-1989)
American defense attorney in the Sleepy Lagoon murder trial .

zoot suit
An exaggerated version of the traditional business suit that became popular with Hispanic, black, white, and Asian youth in the 1930s and early 1940s. Standard zoot-suit elements included long coats with wide padded shoulders and lapels, high-waisted, pleated pants that fit tightly around the ankles, thick-soled shoes, broad-brimmed hats, suspenders, narrow belts, and long watch chains.

CHRONOLOGY

1492
Christopher Columbus discovers the Americas. *See p. 7.*

1521
The Aztec Empire falls to Spanish conquistadores. *See p. 10.*

1533
The Inca Empire is overthrown by Spanish invaders. *See p. 10.*

1542
Spain adopts a set of colonial laws that grants citizenship to Indians in Spanish-controlled lands in the New World. *See p. 13.*

1680
Pueblo Indians rebel against Spanish rule in modern-day New Mexico. *See p. 14.*

1808
The Napoleonic Wars result in a brief French takeover of the Spanish Empire—and several declarations of independence from French-controlled Spanish colonies in South and Central America and the Caribbean. *See p. 15.*

1814
King Ferdinand regains power in Spain. *See p. 16.*

1819
Spain and the United States sign the Adams-Onís Treaty, which transfers ownership of Florida to the United States. *See p. 16.*

1821
Mexico gains independence from Spain. *See p. 16.*

1836
Anglo settlers in Texas declare independence from Mexico. *See p. 18.*

1845
The United States annexes Texas. *See p. 20.*

1846
The dispute over possession of Texas erupts into the Mexican-American War. *See p. 20.*

1847

American forces under General Winfield Scott conquer Mexico City. *See p. 22.*

1848

The Mexican-American War ends with the signing of the Treaty of Guadalupe Hidalgo on February 2, 1848. Under the terms of the treaty, Mexico relinquishes 525,000-square-miles of territory, including all or most of the present-day states of Arizona, California, Colorado, Nevada, New Mexico, Texas, and Utah, as well as parts of Oklahoma, Kansas, and Wyoming. *See p. 22.*

1849

The California Gold Rush brings tens of thousands of Anglo settlers to the West. *See p. 22.*

1853

The United States and Mexico sign the Gadsden Purchase, which transfers another 30,000 square miles of Mexican territory to the United States.

1910

The ten-year Mexican Revolution begins, ushering in years of political and economic upheaval. *See p. 27.*

1929

A U.S. stock market crash triggers the Great Depression. *See p. 31.*

1931

Repatriation programs to deport Mexican Americans or pressure them to return to Mexico begin to appear in California and many other western states. *See p. 33.*

1939

World War II begins.

Culbert Olson is sworn in as governor of California after winning election on a law-and-order platform. *See p. 60.*

1941

The United States enters World War II after Japanese forces attack an American naval base at Pearl Harbor, Hawaii. *See p. 38.*

1942

February 19 — President Franklin D. Roosevelt issues Executive Order 9066, setting in motion the mass internment of Japanese Americans during World War II. *See p. 39.*

April — White marines and sailors assault zoot-suited residents in several Mexican-American and African-American neighborhoods in Oakland, California. *See p. 77.*

August 2 — A Mexican migrant worker named José Díaz is found nearly dead on a rural ranch on the outskirts of Los Angeles. His death a few hours later triggers the so-called Sleepy Lagoon murder investigation and trial. *See p. 53.*

August 4 — The United States launches the Bracero Program to attract Mexican workers to American farms experiencing war-related labor shortages. *See p. 35.*

October 13 — The Sleepy Lagoon trial, officially known as *California v. Zammora et al.*, begins; presided over by Judge Charles W. Fricke, the mass trial features a total of seventeen defendants from Los Angeles's mostly Hispanic 38th Street neighborhood. *See p. 65.*

1943

January 12 — All seventeen defendants in the Sleepy Lagoon murder trial are convicted (twelve on murder charges) and most of them are sent to San Quentin Prison. *See p. 71.*

March — Supporters of the 38th Street defendants form the Sleepy Lagoon Defense Committee (SLDC) to raise funds for appeals of their convictions. *See p. 72.*

May 8 — A race riot breaks out at Venice Beach, California, when white sailors react to a false rumor that a serviceman has been stabbed on the beachfront by zoot-suited Mexican Americans. Hundreds of white sailors and civilians attack Mexican Americans leaving an area dance hall. *See p. 77.*

May 31 — A violent clash between white sailors and zoot suiters in downtown Los Angeles further heightens racial tensions throughout the city. *See p. 78.*

June 3-8 — The so-called Zoot Suit Riots erupt across Los Angeles. Mobs of white servicemen and civilians attack Mexican-American and black civilians (including both zoot suiters and non-zoot suiters). White police officers make little effort to intervene, and in some cases they reportedly contribute to the mayhem with unprovoked attacks on minorities. *See p. 78.*

June 9 — Commanders at area military bases issue explicit orders for personnel to stay out of Los Angeles. *See p. 84.*

June 13 — The McGucken Report is released; it identifies racial prejudice as a major factor in the Zoot Suit Riots. *See p. 88.*

1944

October 2 — The U.S. Second Court of Appeals unanimously reverses all the convictions in *People v. Zammora* and sets aside all the sentences. The Los Angeles District Attorney's Office subsequently decides against pursuing a new trial against the Sleepy Lagoon defendants. *See p. 97.*

October 23 — All the Sleepy Lagoon defendants who were sent to San Quentin Prison are freed. *See p. 99.*

1945

World War II ends and American servicemen return home. *See p. 101.*

1947

California desegregates its public school system. *See p. 108.*

1949

Edward Roybal wins election to the Los Angeles City Council. *See p. 108.*

1954

May 3 — The U.S. Supreme Court announces in *Hernandez v. Texas* that Mexican Americans are a "distinct class" that has the right to protection from discrimination. *See p. 108.*

May 17 — The U.S. Supreme Court issues its landmark *Brown v. Board of Education* decision, which strikes down school segregation across the United States. *See p. 108.*

1960s

The Chicano civil rights movement builds across the United States. *See p. 110.*

1978

The hit play *Zoot Suit*, written and directed by Luis Valdez, premiers in Los Angeles. *See p. 112.*

2005

Antonio R. Villaraigosa wins election to become the first Hispanic mayor of Los Angeles in 130 years. *See p. 121.*

2009

Sonia Sotomayor becomes the first Hispanic justice in the history of the U.S. Supreme Court. *See p. 121.*

SOURCES FOR FURTHER STUDY

"Latino in America." CNN. Retrieved from http://www.cnn.com/SPECIALS/2009/latino.in.america/. This 2009 television special hosted by Soledad O'Brien has been organized for exploration on CNN.com. It includes video interviews, special commentaries, and other special features on various aspects of life in the United States for Hispanic-American individuals, families, and communities. Topics covered range from strong Latino ties to the Catholic Church to the perils that face illegal immigrants.

Library of Congress. "Hispanic Americans." Retrieved from http://www.loc.gov/teachers/classroommaterials/themes/hispanic-americans/index.html. This Web site features a treasure trove of materials on the history of Hispanics in the United States. The collection includes historical maps and photographs, primary source documents, multimedia exhibitions, original essays, and special resources for students.

Pew Research Center. "Pew Hispanic Center." Retrieved from www.pewhispanic.org/. Part of the prestigious Pew Research Center, the Pew Hispanic Center describes itself as a "nonpartisan research organization that seeks to improve understanding of the U.S. Hispanic population and to chronicle Latinos' growing impact on the nation." Its Web site features a wide array of historical and current demographic data on Hispanic Americans, including information on financial, educational, and citizenship trends. The Center also provides coverage of immigration, youth issues, social values, and other high-interest topics.

Rodriguez, Robert. *Great Hispanic-Americans*. Lincolnwood, IL: Publications International, 2005. This richly illustrated book provides brief but informative and colorful biographies of 55 Hispanic Americans who have made important contributions to American society in a wide range of fields.

Sanchez, George J. *Becoming Mexican-American: Ethnicity, Culture, and Identity in Chicano Los Angeles, 1900-1945*. New York: Oxford University Press, 1993. This historical work surveys how Mexican immigrants became an important—if underappreciated—part of Los Angeles during the first half of the twentieth century. The author explores the various ways in which the new arrivals strove to fit into their new home, yet still preserved important parts of their cultural heritage. In the process, they laid the foundation for a new Mexican-American culture in both the city and the state of California.

Thorpe, Helen. *Just Like Us: The True Story of Four Mexican Girls Coming of Age in America.* New York: Scribner, 2009. This engrossing book tells the story of four high school classmates in Denver, Colorado, whose lives are diverging as they prepare for their senior prom. All are the daughters of Mexican immigrants who have lived most of their lives in the United States, but only two of them are living in America legally. Their friendships with one another are tested as they move toward adulthood—and discover that their legal status will exert enormous influence over the lives that each girl can build for herself. In the meantime, the book wrestles with the question of whether the two girls living here illegally have any right to remain in the country where they have grown up.

BIBLIOGRAPHY

Books and Periodicals

Acuña, Rudolfo. *Anything but Mexican: Chicanos in Contemporary Los Angeles.* New York: Verso, 1995.

Aguirre, Frederick P., and Linda Martinez Aguirre. *Undaunted Courage: Mexican-American Patriots of World War II.* Orange, CA: Latino Advocates for Education, 2004.

Alvarez, Luis. *The Power of the Zoot: Youth Culture and Resistance during World War II.* Berkeley: University of California Press, 2008.

Barajas, Frank P. "The Defense Committees of Sleepy Lagoon: A Convergent Struggle against Fascism, 1942-1944." *Aztlán: A Journal of Chicano Studies,* Spring 2006.

del Castillo, Richard Griswold. "The Los Angeles 'Zoot Suit Riots' Revisited: Mexican and Latin American Perspectives." *Mexican Studies/Estudios Mexicanos,* Summer 2000, pp. 367-391.

Escobar, Edward. *Race, Police, and the Making of a Political Identity: Mexican Americans and the Los Angeles Police Department, 1900-1945.* Berkeley: University of California Press, 1999.

Fox, Geoffrey. *Hispanic Nation: Culture, Politics, and the Constructing of Identity.* Secaucus, NJ: Carol Publishing, 1996.

Gonzalez, Juan. *Harvest of Empire: A History of Latinos in America.* New York: Viking, 2000.

Gutiérrez, David G., ed. *The Columbia History of Latinos in the United States since 1960.* New York: Columbia University Press, 2004.

Heide, Rick, ed. *Under the Fifth Sun: Latino Literature from California.* Berkeley, CA: Heyday Books/Santa Clara University, 2002.

Leonard, Kevin Allen. *The Battle for Los Angeles: Racial Ideology and World War II.* Albuquerque: University of New Mexico Press, 2006.

Lynch, John. *The Spanish American Revolutions, 1808-1826* (2nd edition). New York, W. W. Norton & Company, 1986.

Mazón, Mauricio. *The Zoot Suit Riots: The Psychology of Symbolic Annihilation.* Austin: University of Texas Press, 1984.

McWilliams, Carey. *North from Mexico: The Spanish-Speaking People of the United States*. New York: Monthly Review Press, 1961.

Moore, Joan W. *Going Down to the Barrio: Homeboy and Homegirls in Change*. Philadelphia: Temple University Press, 1991.

Pagán, Eduardo Obregón. *Murder at the Sleepy Lagoon: Zoot Suits, Race, and Riot in Wartime L.A.* Chapel Hill: University of North Carolina Press, 2003.

Peiss, Kathy. *Zoot Suit: The Enigmatic Career of an Extreme Style*. Philadelphia: University of Pennsylvania Press, 2011.

Shorris, Earl. *Latinos: A Biography of the People*. New York: W. W. Norton, 1992.

Suro, Roberto. *Strangers Among Us: How Latino Immigration Is Transforming America*. New York: Knopf, 1998.

Valdez, Luis. *Zoot Suit and Other Plays*. Houston: Arte Publico Press, 1992.

Weitz, Mark A. *The Sleepy Lagoon Murder Case: Race Discrimination and Mexican-American Rights*. Lawrence: University Press of Kansas, 2010.

Online Resources

American Experience (PBS). "The Zoot Suit Riots," 2002. Retrieved from www.pbs.org/wgbh/amex/zoot/.

"Latino Civil Rights Timeline, 1903-2006." Teaching Tolerance: A Project of the Southern Poverty Law Center. Retrieved from www.tolerance.org/latino-civil-rights-timeline.

"Zoot Suit Discovery Guide," 2012. Retrieved from www.research.pomona.edu/zootsuit/.

PHOTO AND ILLUSTRATION CREDITS

Cover photo: UCLA Charles E. Young Library Department of Special Collections, Los Angeles Daily News Photographic Archives, Copyright © Regents of the University of California, UCLA Library.

Chapter One: Prints & Photographs Division, Library of Congress, LC-USZ62-47764 (p. 9); Prints & Photographs Division, Library of Congress, LC-USZ62-37993 (p. 11); Carol M. Highsmith Archive, Prints & Photographs Division, Library of Congress, LC-DIG-highsm-12429 (p. 12); © Iberfoto/The Image Works (p. 15); Calabria Design/Copyright © 2012 Omnigraphics, Inc. (p. 17); The Granger Collection, NYC—All rights reserved. (p. 18); © Mary Evans Picture Library/The Image Works (p. 21); Lithograph by Currier & Ives (1871), Prints & Photographs Division, Library of Congress, LC-USZC2-1755 (p. 23).

Chapter Two: Courtesy of United Fruit Company, Unifruitco Magazine, Prints & Photographs Division, Library of Congress, LC-USZ62-101686 (p. 26); The Robert Runyon Photograph Collection (RUN02466), courtesy of The Dolph Briscoe Center for American History, The University of Texas at Austin (p. 29); Los Angeles Public Library Photo Collection (p. 30); Prints & Photographs Division, Library of Congress, LC-USZ62-120535 (p. 32); Leonard Nadel Bracero Photograph Collection, Division of Work & Industry, National Museum of American History, Smithsonian Institution (p. 36); Photograph by U. S. Army Signal Corps, Prints & Photographs Division, Library of Congress, LC-USZ62-133822 (p. 39).

Chapter Three: Photo by Frank Driggs/Frank Driggs Collection/Getty Images (p. 45); Copyright Bettmann/Corbis / AP Images (p. 47); Los Angeles Public Library Photo Collection (pp. 49 and 55).

Chapter Four: UCLA Charles E. Young Research Library Department of Special Collections, Los Angeles Times Photographic Archive, Copyright © Regents of the University of California, UCLA Library (p. 62); Los Angeles Public Library Photo Collection (p. 64); Courtesy of William Shibley (p. 67); Courtesy of University of Southern California, on behalf of the USC Special Collections (p. 68); New York World-Telegram and the Sun Newspaper Collection, Prints & Photographs Division, Library of Congress, LC-USZ62-115739 (p. 70); Copyright Bettmann/Corbis / AP Images (p. 72).

Chapter Five: AP Photo (p. 76); Anthony Potter Collection/Hulton Archive/Getty Images (p. 80); Copyright Bettmann/Corbis / AP Images (pp. 83 and 84); Collection of Fleet Admiral Chester W. Nimitz / U.S. Naval Historical Center Photograph (p. 86).

Chapter Six: UCLA Charles E. Young Research Library Department of Special Collections, Los Angeles Daily News Photographic Archives, Copyright © Regents of the University of California, UCLA Library (p. 93); Copyright Bettmann/Corbis / AP Images (p. 98); Los Angeles Public Library Photo Collection (p. 100); VOCES Oral History Project, University of Texas, Austin (p. 103).

Chapter Seven: Los Angeles Public Library Photo Collection (p. 109); AP Photo/Daniel Goodrich (p. 111); © Universal Pictures/Photofest (p. 112); Statistical Data Tables courtesy of the Pew Hispanic Center / http://www.pewhispanic.org/2012/02/21/statistical-portrait-of-hispanics-in-the-united-states-2010/ (pp. 115, 116, 117, and 119); AP Photo/Frank Wiese (p. 120).

Biographies: Los Angeles Public Library Photo Collection (p. 125); Courtesy of University of Southern California, on behalf of the USC Special Collections (p. 131); UCLA Charles E. Young Research Library Department of Special Collections, Los Angeles Times Photographic Archive, Copyright © Regents of the University of California, UCLA Library (pp. 137 and 141); AP Photo (p. 145); Courtesy of William Shibley (p. 148).

INDEX

M

N

T

U

V

W

X-Y

Z